W9-ASB-774

The 1964
Presidential Election
in the Southwest

AUGUST O. SPAIN   MARVIN HARDER
JOSEPH L. BERND   GEORGE C. ROBERTS
JOHN W. WOOD   KENNETH N. VINES

ARNOLD FOUNDATION MONOGRAPHS
SOUTHERN METHODIST UNIVERSITY
DALLAS, TEXAS

14-202-■ 34

14-3

Arnold Foundation Monographs
XV

ARNOLD FOUNDATION MONOGRAPHS

John M. Claunch, Editor

Other titles in preparation

E
850
.C56

The 1964 Presidential Election In the Southwest

EDITED BY

JOHN M. CLAUNCH

ARNOLD FOUNDATION MONOGRAPHS XV

Published 1966 by

THE ARNOLD FOUNDATION

Southern Methodist University

Dallas, Texas

137421

The 1964 Presidential Election in the Southwest: Editorial Introduction

AUGUST O. SPAIN

Texas Christian University

At the instance of its first President, Oliver Douglas Weeks, of the University of Texas, the newly reactivated Southwestern Political Science Association sponsors the present effort at a regional study of the national Presidential election of 1964. The sponsoring resolution was adopted at the Easter-season 1964 annual meeting in conjunction with the Southwestern Social Science Association in Dallas, Texas. Agreement was reached with John M. Claunch, Southern Methodist University, representing the Arnold Foundation, to undertake publication. An editorial board was named, comprising: August O. Spain, Texas Christian University, as chairman; Isabel Hunt, Midwestern University; and James R. Jensen, University of Houston. The editorial board recruited a team of five writers, one for each state in the region, to do the study and report: Joseph L. Bernd, Southern Methodist University (Texas); John W. Wood, University of Oklahoma (Oklahoma); Marvin A. Harder, University of Wichita (Kansas); George C. Roberts, University of Arkansas (Arkansas); and Kenneth N. Vines, Tulane University (Louisiana).

Through considerable correspondence and one effort at a consultative conference in Chicago in September of 1964, an attempt was made to achieve a degree of consensus upon substantive content and methods of analysis and evaluation without adopting any prescription of rigid uniformity. It was hoped that both constants and variables in the Presidential politics of the community might be identified and measured or evaluated, as well as significant features of campaign strategy, organization, and activity; candidates and factional roles; interplay between national and state races; critical issues; the influence of interest groups and voter blocs; party regularity and the swing vote; the liberal-conservative alignment; and the diverse impacts of the Negro problem, urbanization, and industrialization. In contrast to some earlier studies, notably the celebrated nationally cooperative project of the American Political Science Association in 1952, chief attention and concern were to be directed to the general election races and results rather than to nominating politics—without however entirely neglecting the latter. Professors Bernd and Vines were especially helpful in formulating suggestions as to the kind of data and the use of quantitative materials that would facilitate comparability from state to state throughout the region. Certainly participants were interested in finding any statistical correlates implicit in the election results between the human behavior on the one hand and ecological factors on the other. Ultimately guidelines were circulated to all the authors.

Although alternative conceptions of the Southwestern region were considered, and some impulse felt to include several other states (especially New Mexico and Arizona and possibly Missouri), it was finally decided to confine the study to Texas, Oklahoma, Kansas, Arkansas, and Louisiana. These were the states most substantially reflective of the membership of the organization. Occasional participation by colleagues from other states did not alter their principal involvement elsewhere in other regional associations. Whether or not such identification of the region produces a Southwest of scientific delineation is doubtful, but practical considerations prevailed.

This maiden effort at a cooperative project on the Presidential election in the Southwest yields some very interesting and enlightening analyses and interpretations. And it would be well in reading these state-by-state accounts to keep the national picture of 1964 clearly in mind. The campaign itself was one of unusual interest to students of American politics. The clash on several big issues was clear cut, a rarity in 20th century elections; and matters of foreign and domestic policy loomed large to the cognoscenti at least. The candidates were colorful and occasionally dramatic. The parties and other organizational effort thrown into the struggle were as big or bigger, as energetic and free-spending as ever. Campaign strategists, the press, the pollsters, and the electronic media hustled about their appointed tasks. And local and state power structures weighed their choices, soon committing their support in the confederating process of quadrennial alignment. The "mystic maze" was at work. Much of the unfolding story followed accustomed paces.

But there were differences. The great parties nominated later than usual, and the campaign was shorter and perhaps more intense. Most fascinating was the bid by the Republican Party to

place its chips boldly on a candidate from the right wing, depart-
ing sharply from theretofore accepted strategy in the two-party
system of seeking votes from the broad middle of the American
political spectrum. Conservative elements, disgruntled with domi-
nation by the "establishment" of Easterners and moderates, wrested
control away, and chose in Goldwater an "unashamed and un-
afraid" temperamental conservative who offered a sharp alternative to the electorate. They blamed the now rejected leadership for
the defeat in 1960 by a Democratic candidate more than normally
vulnerable to attack; and they were titillated by the notion
(sparked perhaps by the "newer conservatism" of extremist groups
and campus youth) that "silent conservatives," who had presumably abstained previously in scorn at the choice between tweedle-
dee and tweedle-dum, might be moved to turn out in large numbers. Despite some vacillating straddles, Goldwater did join issue
frontally with the opposing candidate, the Democratic national
leadership, and the evolving pattern of national policy—in part a
bipartisan pattern. To some, it appeared that he took issue with
the trend of the times and even the nature of the world in which
we live.

Johnson was heir, of course, to the New Deal-Fair Deal-New
Frontier background. But he was also blessed with a personal
image, achieved by skilfull tight-rope walking since 1948, of
moderation and responsibility not unmixed with elements of conservatism. Moreover, the image included masterly craftsmanship
as a legislative leader—proved out in the year under the mantle
of the martyred Kennedy. He appeared to offer peace, prosperity,
and surer navigation along the mainstream of American life. His
campaign exploited the strategy of superior place: his was the
party in power; and it was the party of the majority of American
voters, however compounded of minorities. He promised a continuation of much national consensus forged for a generation by
the emergent necessities of an urban, industrialized, and now
nuclear world. The prospect inspired more confidence than the
impulsive, not to say compulsive, nostalgic negativism of his opponent. His picture of the Great Society appealed to many of
the old New Dealers while his record and style of leadership re-
assured many of the middle class and business gentry. Potential
Republican defectors were artfully wooed away, whether offended
by the political extremism, not to say, vengeful temper of the
Goldwater crowd, or fearful of sharp redirection of national policy

in uncertain times. For all of the patrioteer drum-beating, the popular mood was not ready for Armageddon. "Daddy-ism"—something for everybody without too seriously rocking the boat—was to prevail.

In the biggest national turn-out of voters in all time, the election results gave Johnson a resounding victory—a "landslide." He won 61.3 percent of the votes cast, the largest popular majority ever. His electoral college majority was second only to that of Roosevelt in 1936. Goldwater had won only six states, five of them in the deep South and his own Arizona by a narrow margin. Johnson carried all the other states, including such rock-ribbed New England states as Vermont (first time since the Civil War) and New Hampshire as well as such Republican stalwarts of the mid-American breadbasket as Kansas and Nebraska.

Arizona favorite-son sentiment undoubtedly enabled him to squeak by in his home state, but Goldwater breached the Solid South most emphatically. Louisiana, Mississippi, Alabama, Georgia, and South Carolina responded to his promise to retard the "Negro revolution" and to take a states rights stand. The "solid" South no longer existed. But across the country the "silent conservatives" did not emerge as an electoral factor, if they ever existed. Apparently Goldwater lost many of the "undecided" and defecting "responsible" Republicans; the latter seemingly engaged in extensive ticket-splitting.

Johnson won his greatest support in the big industrial states of the North, compounded of metropolitan machines, labor and minority blocs, and the Negroes. Even the gray-flannel-suit crowd of surburbia and exurbia in the North and East gave him a substantial vote. In much of rural America, notably in the Midwest, he rolled up an unprecedented count, possibly for fear by agrarians of loss of farm price supports or of weakening of the rural electrification program. Outside the deep South the "front lash" at least neutralized if it did not exceed the "back lash." Several analysts credit Johnson with carrying some local candidates into office on his "coattails," as Governor Kerner in Illinois and Robert Kennedy into the U. S. Senate from New York.

In the Southwest, as the present study demonstrates, the national trends were shared, but with difference in detail. For one thing, the voter turn-out was lighter than the national performance. Rain in Kansas and racial barriers to the polls in Louisiana may well have contributed to the result; but the still agrarian, not to say, provincial character of the culture of the region held to a slower pace as usual, even though the gross total vote in several of the states exceeded that of 1960 and constituted an all-time high. Also among the five states the four that went Democratic gave Johnson a smaller majority than that across the country. Only in his home state of Texas did his popular majority of 63 percent exceed the national average of 61 per cent. And, except for Harris in Oklahoma who defeated a popular football coach for the U. S. Senate, Johnson does not appear to have carried Democrats into office on his "coattails"; Bernd rejects this possibility in the case of Yarborough's race for the Senate in Texas. In fact, Governor Connally in that state swept into another term by a ten percent greater popular majority than his chief on the ticket.

In Kansas the defection of possibly ten percent of normally Republican "identifiers" carried the election for Johnson, and made it a "deviating" election. Republican candidates, however, carried all of the Congressional districts, the governorship and all other state administrative offices, and firm control of both state legislative houses. For all but the Presidential ticket, it was a "reinstating" or sustaining election. Republicans defecting from Goldwater apparently did a lot of ticket-splitting to remain Republican at home. Harder concludes that the historical preference for the Republican Party has been little affected, and is not likely to be unless and until major change in the social and economic character of the community occurs.

Such basic realignment may well have been clinched in Louisiana, at the other extreme of political behavior in the region in 1964, not because of transformation in the local social and economic order, but because tenacious loyalty to it defies the national will to change in the field of race relations—a purpose made all the clearer by the son of a neighboring state who has "plunged" for civil rights legislation. However deviating from the older tradition of the Solid South, Vines finds that the results in Louisiana sustain recent trends there. The 1960 vote for Kennedy was the "deviating" election. Of the five states included in the present study, here is the only one in which the racial issue appears to have been determining.

In Texas, Oklahoma, and Arkansas, the Democratic victory followed form and the forecasters' predictions. On the Presidential level, it was a "reinstating" election in Oklahoma, and a sustaining election in Texas and Arkansas. Possibly the Catholicism of Kennedy was all that prevented Oklahoma from having returned to the Democratic fold at the same time her two neighbors did. The "democracy" of Oklahoma and Arkansas appears to remain more rural in orientation than in Texas where Bernd finds the big swing to the Democratic camp (as compared to the 1960 vote) to have occurred in the big metropolitan areas. The big four cities there reversed a recent post-World War II trend to Republicanism. Harder notes some Democratic inroads in the two largest metropolitan areas in Kansas. By contrast Wood finds Republican strength in the two largest cities in Oklahoma largely to have held on. In Arkansas and Louisiana the urban factor tended to remain indecisive.

In this region the Negro vote, while it went heavily for Johnson, does not seem to have contributed importantly to the winning margin. Relatively small in size in Texas, Oklahoma, and Kansas, it did not seem to turn out heavily in Arkansas, although Roberts discerns no administrative interference. Possibly the permissive situation was still strange, of too recent date. In Louisiana Vines finds some correlation between the size of the anti-Johnson vote and the parishes of heavy Negro population, a result explicable only in terms of continuing hobbling of Negro access to the polls.

In the case of Texas, in addition to other factors accounting for the Democratic triumph, Bernd develops an ingenious "heartland" theory—an interpretation in terms of geographic proximity to the Johnson ranch (by Congressional districts) related to reasonable anticipation of benefits in the way of federal patronage. For Arkansas, Roberts presents an excellent picture of the campaign as party rivalry between two internally uncomfortable coalitions of personalities and factions; he characterizes such politics as those of a modified two-party system functioning like a one-party system.

If the future should witness a strengthening of national political consensus under Democratic leadership, among the states of this region Texas would appear to lead the way, followed more slowly by Arkansas and Oklahoma. Kansas remains doubtful, if not opposed. And Louisiana turns sharply aside. Amidst all the reshuffling of 1964, there are signs of continuing Republican strength, even of gain in some localities of the region; but what they portend for the two-party system remains veiled in the future.

The 1964 Presidential Election In Texas

Southern Methodist University

In a perceptive paragraph which remains remarkably up-to-date after fifteen years, the late V. O. Key identified the most vital of Texas political arguments:

> In Texas the vague outlines of a politics are emerging in which irrelevancies are pushed into the background and people divide broadly along liberal and conservative lines. A modified class politics seems to be evolving, not primarily because of an upthrust of the masses that compels men of substance to unite in self-defense, but because of the personal insecurity of men suddenly made rich who are fearful lest they lose their wealth. . . .[1]

When hyperbole and the Texas brand of conservatism are combined, as often they are, in the editorials and letter columns of some newspapers, it is difficult for the reader to escape the conviction that the conservatives are sweeping the Lone Star State. Conservatives, it is true, do win more often than they lose. No liberal has been elected Governor since James V. Allred won in the early days of the New Deal. But when liberal candidates are well known and adequately financed, the results are often close.[2]

An observer with only local auguries to guide him might have anticipated another cliff-hanger in the 1964 Texas presidential election. After all, the Goldwater drive for the White House was begun by Texas Republicans,[3] and Texas money reputedly fuels much of the conservatism and ultra-conservatism of American politics. What then produced the Johnson sweep of Texas in 1964? Did friends and neighbors vote for a native son? Was "white backlash" evident in the East Texas black belt? Did the German counties desert their traditional Republican alignment? How did Negro and Latin-American minorities vote in Texas? Why did the metropolitan areas of the state swing to the Democratic candidate for the first time since before the Eisenhower victories? Statistics

* In revising this study prior to publication, the author has benefited from critical suggestions offered by colleagues in the Social Science Division at S.M.U. and by Dan Weiser, Secretary of the Dallas County Democratic Committee. The defects of the paper are attributable solely to the author.

alone cannot answer such questions, but an analysis of the election returns and other indices may offer some valid clues, either positive or negative.[4]

The purpose of this paper, after recounting briefly some major events of the campaign, is to test questions like those noted in the 1964 election.*

I. THE 1964 PRESIDENTIAL ELECTION IN TEXAS

In 1964 the Texas choices for the presidential nomination were never in doubt. Johnson was a native son and Goldwater was the darling of the state Republican organization.[5]

The absence of effective opposition was symbolized at the state convention when a lady in the balcony waved a lone Scranton banner in futile defiance of a sea of Goldwater enthusiasts.

Issues and Publicity in the 1964 Presidential Campaign. In Texas, as elsewhere in the country, Republican publicity emphasized the "Bobby Baker" scandal and other evidence of alleged moral delinquency in the national government. As election day neared, Republicans in Texas attacked Democratic vice presidential nominee, Hubert Humphrey. Full page ads in the press charged that Humphrey, who denied it, favored admission of Communist China to the U.N. As a co-founder and vice president of Americans for Democratic Action, Humphrey was charged with other sins of liberalism. Except for senatorial candidate George Bush who attacked it, few Texas Republicans emphasized the Civil Rights Act of 1964. The Democrats seemed happy to play down the issue.

Goldwater entered Texas six times and appeared in fifteen cities. He focused on the "moral" issue, attacked centralization of political power, and defended himself against charges of "extremism." The President came for conferences at the LBJ Ranch, but he made only one campaign tour in Texas. During the final weekend before November 3, he appeared in Houston with Senator Yarborough and in Austin with Governor Connally. He defended his record, attacked Republican "irresponsibility," and urged the election of the entire Democratic ticket.

The circulation of "smear literature" was perhaps the most widespread in the history of the country or the state. Most widely circulated in Texas was *A Texan Looks At Lyndon* by J. Evetts

---

* The author was assisted in the collection of data by Mary K. Peterson and Mary Galen Thomas, two students at Southern Methodist University.

Haley of Canyon. The book recounts several longstanding charges against Johnson, including the allegation that his 1948 senatorial nomination was made possible by fraudulent ballots in South Texas and that improper governmental influence had been exerted on behalf of the Austin television station owned by the Johnson family. The factual data in the volume are overlaid with assumptions which are unwarranted by evidence: liberalism is equated with communism and treason; motives, about which facts are lacking, are held to be dishonest; LBJ is endlessly guilty by association. Similar techniques are evident in other campaign documents: John A. Stormer's *None Dare Call It Treason* and Phyllis Schlafly's *A Choice Not An Echo.*

The principal anti-Goldwater smear was a publication called *Fact* which charged that "1,189 Psychiatrists Say Goldwater Is Psychologically Unfit To Be President!" In this magazine boyish pranks are equated with paranoia, a youthful illness due to overwork is "a nervous breakdown," and political views (unsound perhaps) are regarded as symptoms of mental and emotional incompetence. Behind the facade of medical expertise, the psychiatrists level a political indictment in the guise of medical opinion. In keeping with traditional practice, most of the smear publicity was not openly endorsed by the major parties themselves.[6]

The Press. A campaign ad in the *Dallas Morning News* listed forty-seven Texas papers, mostly dailies, which were supporting the Johnson-Humphrey ticket in the 1964 election. Many of these papers had backed Eisenhower in his two races and Nixon in 1960. Almost none was regarded as "liberal." The principal papers of the state were heavily represented. A majority of these papers did not support Senator Yarborough in his bid for Senate reelection. The *Dallas News,* in recent years a champion of Texas "conservatism" and a caustic critic of the mainstream of federal policy, withheld support from Goldwater and Johnson despite the fact that the Goldwater position on major issues was substantially consistent with the various stands of the paper.[7]

Prominent Personal and Organizational Support. Two Texans, formerly members of the Eisenhower cabinet, supported President Johnson. Mrs. Oveta Culp Hobby had been the first secretary of Health, Education, and Welfare, and Robert Anderson had been Secretary of the Treasury and Secretary of the Army. The Anderson endorsement of Johnson was especially valued and was publicized by the Democrats as symbolizing the pro-Johnson shifts of men in finance and business. Another key Johnson backer, recruited from the ranks of recent boosters of Republican candidates on the presidential level, was former Governor Allan Shivers. Shivers, thrice elected as a Democrat, had abandoned Adlai Stevenson in his two campaigns for President primarily because of the Stevenson stand opposing state ownership of the oil-rich tidelands. As Texas Governor, Shivers brought over much of his own personal organization to Eisenhower and his contacts were also valuable to Nixon in 1960 after Shivers had left office. This support, especially significant in rural counties, was understandably crucial to the Republicans who had no state-wide organization in what had been traditionally a one-party state. Shivers has been a leader of considerable personal attraction to conservative Democrats, and his failure to support Goldwater was a severe blow to the latter. Although he did not actively campaign for Johnson, Shivers issued a public endorsement of the President. His support contributed to the number and enthusiasm of "Businessmen for Johnson," whose endorsement was important throughout Texas.

The Republicans in 1964 did feature an organization of "Democrats for Goldwater," although it lacked the leadership of well-known personalities, as when Shivers headed the "Democrats for Nixon" in 1960. More prominent in 1964 were "Republicans for Johnson," which included former Dallas Republican leaders Maurice Carlson and Edward T. Dicker. Liberal groups were also more effective with a Texan in the White House. PASO, the Political Association of Spanish-Speaking Organizations, headed by Commissioner Albert Pena of San Antonio, the AFL-CIO headed by Hank Brown, and various Negro political groups were active in drives to sell poll taxes and to get out the vote. An association of organized labor, Negroes, and Latin-Americans called "the Coalition" was able to coordinate some activities of the liberal minorities.

Texan in the White House. The Johnson story is well-known and need not be repeated here. Despite his early New Deal associations, the LBJ image in the decade prior to 1964 appeared ambiguous to many, and reaction ranged from friendly to hostile among both conservatives and liberals. His tactics had changed to meet circumstances. In 1965 he formed an alliance with liberals to secure support for his presidential aspirations at the national convention. In 1960 he allied with conservatives to obtain control of the delegation to the national convention at the expense of liberals. But when he was chosen by John F. Kennedy to be his vice presidential nominee, Johnson repudiated conservative stands in favor of the liberal platform of the national party. In the meantime he had played a major role in the passage of the Civil Rights Acts of 1957 and 1960. In his home state his role had been to play the ends against each other while he occupied the middle ground.

Johnson was often damned in the editorial columns of the *Dallas Morning News,* while the liberal *Texas Observer,* on the opposite side of the political spectrum, regarded him with guarded suspicion or outright hostility. In 1960 he aroused criticism because he was simultaneously a candidate for Vice President and U. S. Senator. A popular jingle with his critics was "Double your pleasure, double your fun, scratch Lyndon twice." But when the votes were counted, the Kennedy-Johnson ticket had carried Texas by forty-six thousand votes (51 per cent) and LBJ had been re-elected to the Senate by almost four hundred thousand.

Johnson's 1960 senatorial opponent was John Tower, then running his first statewide campaign and not yet well-known to the voters. Many Texans refused to believe that LBJ was really popular with the home folks, but others argued that the Johnson critics of right and left were not representative of the majority sentiment. On the other hand, a prominent political figure, who had held a high position in the Kennedy-Johnson campaign of 1960 in Texas, summed up LBJ's campaign role in these words: "I think that from the Texas-Louisiana boundary to the Atlantic seaboard, Johnson's presence on the ticket was of inestimable value to the Kennedy success, but in Texas it probably cost us a hundred thousand votes."

II. Analysis of the 1964 Presidential Election in Texas

Support for a Native Texan. Because of the serious grounds for doubting the popularity of the President in his home state, it seems appropriate to begin the analysis of the 1964 election with an inquiry concerning this point.

As indicated by Table 1, the Johnson victory in 1964 was a sweeping one, surpassing other Democratic performers in recent years. Does this indicate the appeal of a native son? *Hypothesis*: Texas favored Johnson more strongly than the country and his Texas vote surpassed that of other recent Democratic presidential candidacies because he is a native son of Texas.

Statistical verification or refutation of this hypothesis may be obtained by comparing the Texas vote for Johnson with the national vote for him and by comparing the 1964 returns with those for other recent presidential elections.

Table 2 indicates that the Johnson vote in Texas was two per cent larger than that in the country as a whole, but the same type of measurement reveals that in the two Eisenhower-Stevenson elections, Texas also favored the Democratic presidential nominee by 2.2 and 2.1 per cent above the national figures. Therefore, Adlai Stevenson, who was not a native son of Texas, actually has a slight advantage over Johnson, according to this criterion. The statistical measure does not offer evidence supporting the "native son" hypothesis, but it does suggest that Texas had tended in recent years to be slightly more Democratic than the country despite two-party tendencies in presidential elections.

TABLE 1
Major Party Vote: Recent Presidential Elections†

Year	Democratic Vote popular — %		Counties Carried	Republican Vote popular — %		Counties Carried
1948*	821,984	(66.3)	245	303,507	(24.5)	9
1952	969,227	(46.8)	116	1,102,878	(53.2)	138
1956	859,958	(44.3)	120	1,080,619	(55.7)	134
1960	1,167,932	(51.0)	172	1,121,699	(49.0)	82
1964	1,663,185	(63.4)	238	958,566	(36.6)	16

† 1964 official returns were furnished by the office of Crawford C. Martin, Secretary of State, State of Texas. Other totals (except for 1948 Democratic vote) are from Texas Research Project Committee, *Texas Votes* (Austin: Institute of Public Affairs, The University of Texas: 1964), pp. 5-20. The 1948 Democratic total is erroneously stated, but has been corrected from the county returns in the same volume.

* The vote for the States Rights Democrats in 1948 was 113,759 (9.2%).

TABLE 2
Democratic Tendency In Texas Voting: Recent Presidential Elections†

Year	United States Democratic Vote	Texas Democratic Vote	Deviation Percentage
1952	44.6%	46.8%	+2.2%
1956	42.2	44.3	+2.1
1960	50.1	51.0	+0.9
1964	61.4	63.4	+2.0

† The percentages are for major parties only. Vote for minor parties is excluded from consideration.

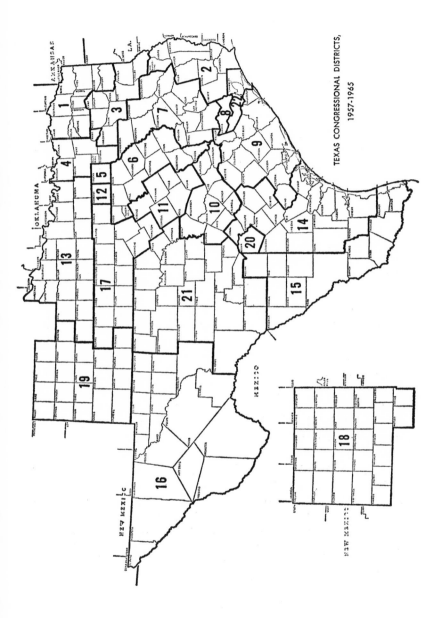

TEXAS CONGRESSIONAL DISTRICTS, 1957-1965

Hypothesis: While the appeal of a native son is not statistically evident in the comparison of gross averages (Table 2), regional vote analysis within the state may suggest that the presence of a Texas friend and neighbor in the White House did influence the 1964 voting.

The Heartland Theory. A heartland theory may be examined (see Table 3) if congressional districts are assembled in two groups according to their remoteness from or proximity to the LBJ Ranch. Assume that the heartland is composed of the 4th, 6th, 7th, 9th, 10th, 11th, 13th, 14th, 15th, 17th, and 21st congressional districts. The periphery is composed of the districts bordering Louisiana on the east and New Mexico on the west. It includes the 1st, 2nd, 3rd, 16th, 18th, and 19th districts. Because of factors of special interest, the five metropolitan districts are treated separately. These are the 5th (Dallas County), 8th and 22nd (Harris County), the 12th (Tarrant County), and the 20th (Bexar County). In Table 3 the districts are ranked according to the net pro-Democratic change from the 1960 election to the 1964 election. Three of the districts in the highest quartile of change are in the heartland group, and two districts of the highest quartile are in the metropolitan group. Four of the districts in the peripheral group are included among the lowest quartile of change, one is in the next lowest quartile, and the final district is in the second highest quartile. Only one district in the lowest quartile is included in the heartland group. No district in the metro group is found in the lowest quartile. The average rank position of the heartland group is 9.5; for the metro group the average is 6.75; and for the peripheral group the average is 16.6.

When the districts are ranked according to percentage of Democratic support in 1964 (see also Table 3), the evidence in favor of the heartland theory is even stronger. The average for the heartland districts is 6.45; for the metro group 14.5; and for the peripheral districts 17.0. Thus the evidence strongly suggests that support for President Johnson tended to vary inversely with the distance from the LBJ Ranch. What factors motivated Texas voters to support a friend and neighbor? Interviews suggested four factors to account for this support: (1) Identification with President Johnson because he is a Texan; (2) Anti-Goldwater sentiment; (3) Identification of President Johnson with general prosperity; (4) The belief, particularly evident in the area close to the LBJ Ranch, that the Johnson presidency would mean economic advantages to the locality.

When the 1960 returns are tested according to the heartland theory, the heartland group averages a rank position of 7.9; the peripheral group average 12.7; and the metro group averages 7.0. Thus the heartland districts were the most favorably disposed toward the Democrats when John F. Kennedy headed the ticket, but the support was relatively stronger in 1964, as indicated by the average of 6.45 as compared with 7.9 in 1960. The relative decline in the position of the peripheral districts is more dramatic, from 12.7 to 17.0. The metro districts have shown the strongest pro-Democratic change, from 17.0 to 14.5.

White Backlash in East Texas. The figures suggest another question worthy of attention. Is the relatively low degree of Democratic support in the East Texas districts related to racial issues, for it is in East Texas that the highest proportions of the Texas Negro population is found? *Hypothesis*: The Johnson support in East Texas was reduced by "white backlash." In its traditional values, in its large proportion of Negro population, and in its emphasis on an agricultural economy, East Texas shares characteristics typical of the "deep South." The region includes three congressional districts which border Louisiana—the 1st, 2nd, and 3rd. All except two of the counties in these districts contain more than ten per cent of Negro population.[8] If it is appropriate to define "white backlash" as voter reaction against the drive for desegregation and for other forms of equality, including those required by the Civil Rights Act of 1964, it is logical to assume that this type of voter reaction would be anti-Johnson and pro-Goldwater in 1964. After all, Johnson, as President, led the fight for the passage of the act and Senator Goldwater opposed its final passage. One generalization, noted by students of racial issues, is that anti-Negro voting patterns tend to be strongest among whites where Negro population is largest. The fact that Senator Goldwater carried five states of the "deep South" is consistent with this generalization. East Texas is adjacent to Louisiana in which Goldwater received 56.8 per cent of the two-party vote.

Table 3 shows that two of the three districts were in the lowest quartile of Democratic support in 1964 and the other was in the third quartile. By contrast the 1960 positions were first quartile, second quartile, and lowest quartile (for the third district which has consistent Republican tendencies). When net change is examined, it appears that the Democratic vote was not reduced, as

compared with 1960, but that the increase was much less than
that in the balance of the state. All three East Texas districts are
in the lowest quartile in terms of pro-Johnson change. The percentage change in the Democratic vote in Texas is +12.4; the
change for the three districts is +4.9. The 1960 average for the

TABLE 3

Democratic Vote As A Percentage of Major Party Vote,
1960 and 1964* (By Congressional Districts)

Cong. Dists.‡	1960 Vote %		1964 Vote %		Net Change %	
1	58.3	(7)†	63.8	(12)†	+ 5.5	(20)†
2	59.1	(5)	62.6	(16)	+ 3.5	(21)
3	47.4	(16)	53.0	(21)	+ 5.6	(19)
4	57.4	(8)	72.2	(4)	+14.8	(6)
5	37.3	(21)	54.8	(19)	+17.5	(3)
6	59.5	(4)	72.3	(3)	+12.8	(11½)
7	56.7	(9)	64.3	(11)	+ 7.6	(16)
8 & 22 **	46.9	(17)	59.6	(17)	+12.7	(13)
9	56.3	(10)	67.0	(9)	+10.7	(15)
10	58.5	(6)	71.3	(5)	+12.8	(11½)
11	61.8	(2)	75.9	(1)	+14.1	(7½)
12	44.9	(19)	63.2	(14)	+18.3	(1)
13	53.7	(12)	70.7	(6)	+17.0	(4)
14	59.9	(3)	73.4	(2)	+13.5	(9)
15	63.2	(1)	70.5	(7)	+ 7.2	(17)
16	49.7	(15)	56.5	(18)	+ 6.8	(18)
17	50.2	(14)	66.9	(10)	+16.7	(5)
18	38.9	(20)	53.0	(20)	+14.1	(7½)
19	50.6	(13)	63.0	(15)	+12.4	(14)
20	54.1	(11)	67.1	(8)	+13.0	(10)
21	45.7	(18)	63.7	(13)	+18.0	(2)
State	51.0		63.4		+12.4	

* Figures for the 1960 election are taken from United States Bureau of the Census, *Congressional District Data Book*, (Washington, D.C.: U.S. Government Printing
Office, 1962), pp. 483-492. Figures for the 1964 election are computed from the
official returns from Secretary of State Crawford C. Martin.

‡ In 1952 the Democrats won a majority in the following districts: 1st, 2nd, 3rd,
4th, 6th, 7th, 10th, 11th, 13th. In 1956 the Democrats won the 1st, 4th, 6th, 11th,
13th, 19th.

† The figures in parentheses represent the rank order of each vote column.

** The 22nd district was created in 1957 from the southern portion of Harris
County (formerly the 8th district).

three districts was +3.9 compared with the state Democratic percentage. The Democratic average in the three districts in 1964 is —3.6 compared with the Democratic percentage for the state.

The picture becomes clearer if the estimated Negro vote of the region is considered separately and 1964 performance is compared with that of 1960. In the earlier year East Texas Negro votes split about seventy-five per cent for Kennedy to twenty-five per cent for Nixon. Evidence for 1964 reveals that Johnson received upwards of ninety-five per cent of Negro votes in virtually all areas. Consequently, an estimated ninety-six per cent for the East Texas districts is probably low. There is no evidence that Negro voting in East Texas was limited by intimidation or other invidious factors. It is, therefore, reasonable to assume that Negroes actually cast ballots in roughly the same proportion of those qualified to vote as did white persons.[9] In 1960 an estimated 35,931 Negroes cast ballots in the three districts. In 1964 the estimated Negro vote in the three districts was 59,410. Using these estimates and the known division of the vote in the three districts, the following picture may be shown:

	Democrats			*Republicans*		
	White	Negro	Total	White	Negro	Total
1960:	112,000	26,948	138,948	103,284	8,983	112,267
1964:	109,878	57,034	166,912	109,654	2,376	112,030

Based on these figures, the Republican vote among whites increased by 6,370 (6.2 per cent) compared with a state decline of more than two hundred thousand (19.0 per cent) of all votes. The decline in East Texas in total Republican vote was 237 (0.21 per cent)! Among East Texas Democrats, the white vote actually declined by 2,122 (1.9 per cent) compared with a statewide increase of five hundred thousand (42.8 per cent) in the total of Democratic ballots. The figures reveal that Democratic gains in East Texas totals—27,964 (20.1 per cent)—were due entirely to heavily increased Negro balloting. The figures strongly suggest the presence of a backlash effect among white voters in East Texas.

Another statistical item suggests restraint on pro-Democratic tendencies in East Texas and its probable relationship to white backlash: only seven of the 254 Texas counties actually produced a percentage increase in the Republican county vote in 1964, as compared with the 1960 vote. Four of these seven counties (Bowie, Orange, Panola, and San Augustine) are in East Texas.[10] In past performance they have been strongly Democratic.

The evidence of a reduction in the Democratic voting tendencies of white persons in East Texas is clear, but its dimensions are small. If the reduction is due to white backlash, the contrast to the rest of the "deep South" is quite sharp. Goldwater gains in the latter areas were of huge proportions. The contrast suggests sub-regional influences on voter motivations and values. Traditionally, the "deep South" states have focused on racial politics. East Texas, however, is part of a state system in which, as V. O. Key noted, the emphasis has been on economics. Still other values no doubt contributed to a pattern in East Texas which markedly reduced the effect of racial politics without eliminating it.

Correlation of Democratic Tendency with Negro and Latin-American Proportion of Population. Negro support of LBJ may mean a positive correlation between a high proportion of Negro population and Democratic voting tendency. Yet, as we have seen in our analysis of East Texas, the existence of an issue involving the Negro tends to produce anti-Democratic tendencies among whites in the same community. *Hypothesis*: The Democratic vote of Texas congressional districts in the 1964 presidential election varies directly with the proportion of Negro population. To test this hypothesis the Pearson coefficient of correlation was used.[11] The mean for the Negro population of the twenty-two congressional districts is 13.0 per cent and the standard deviation is 8.61.[12, 13] The mean for Democratic vote is 64.7 per cent and the standard deviation is 6.96. The coefficient of correlation is —.077, thus indicating that the finding is negative. Democratic vote clearly does not vary directly with the proportion of Negro population, but the minus coefficient is not large enough to suggest a definite white voter reaction against Negro support of the Democrats. In other words, since whites heavily outnumber Negroes, the negative coefficient would be very large if whites voted against Johnson because Negroes voted for him. Such an effect would produce a substantial negative correlation, as no doubt returns from other "deep South" areas would reveal.

Since the heartland theory, presented earlier, includes within the pro-Johnson heartland the areas heavily populated by persons of Latin-American descent and since this vote is presumably attracted to the Democratic Party by ties of economic interest and religious affiliation, it is possible that positive correlation exists between Latin-American proportion of population and Democratic tendency. *Hypothesis*: The Democratic vote of Texas congressional districts in the 1964 presidential election varies directly with the proportion of persons with Spanish surnames. The mean for the proportion of persons with Spanish surnames in the districts is 12.7 per cent; the standard deviation is 16.68 The mean for the Democratic vote is 64.7 per cent and the standard deviation is 6.96. The Pearson coefficient of correlation is +.253. The figure suggests that the proportion of Spanish surnames is statistically related in a direct way to the Democratic tendency in the vote. Yet the figure is not sufficiently high to preclude other variables as correlates of this party's support.

Use of the Pearson coefficient, above, fails to reveal positive correlation between Negro population and Democratic tendency. Correlation between Spanish surnames and Democratic tendency is positive and significant, but it fails to explain Democratic tendencies in congressional districts in which neither Negroes nor Latins are numerous.

Impact of the "Religious Issue" in 1960 and of its Removal in 1964. A tentative and partial explanation of fluctuations in presidential voting among white Protestants[14] may be discerned if attention is focused on the so-called religious issue. *Hypothesis*: In traditionally Democratic counties, populated largely by white Protestants, the party strength was reduced in 1960, when the presidential candidate was John F. Kennedy, a Roman Catholic. Democratic tendency returned in 1964, when the Democrats nominated President Johnson, a Protestant.

In 1960 fifty-six counties in Texas showed an upsurge of Republican voting percentage, although Kennedy won narrowly in the state. Not one of these counties is in the highest quartile in terms of Negro or of Latin population, and a majority of them are in the lowest quartile. Forty-nine of these counties are in the two Panhandle congressional districts (the 18th and 19th) or in the 13th district. In 1964 forty-three of these counties swung toward Johnson by a margin of change larger than the state average (12.4 per cent). Twelve counties of the group swung toward Johnson by a margin less than the state average. Only one of the fifty-six counties actually showed an increased Republican tendency. The evidence suggests that the trend in 1960 was transitory in effect.

In South Texas, on the other hand, the most marked changes in party alignment occurred in 1952 and 1960. Counties of large

Latin and Catholic population proportion swung to Eisenhower in his two elections, but returned to the Democratic fold in 1960.

Analysis of the behavior of these counties in 1960 and 1964 suggests the importance of the religious issue in the former contest and of its absence in the latter. The temporary defection of the North Texas counties from the Democratic fold is, however,

TABLE 4.
Democratic Areas of Persistent Strength in Presidential Elections:
Counties in Highest Quartile of Party Vote—1952, '56, '60, '64.

County	Cong. Dist.	County	Cong. Dist.	County	Cong. Dist.
Bastrop [n]	10th	Duval [s, o]	14th	Knox [c]	13th
Bell [c]	11th	Falls [c, n]	11th	LaSalle [s]	15th
Brooks [s, o]	14th	Fannin [c]	4th	Mitchell [c]	19th
Burleson [c, n]	10th	Fisher [c]	17th	Navarro [c, n]	6th
Clay [o]	13th	Foard [c]	13th	Robertson [n]	6th
Cottle [c]	18th	Franklin	1st	San Jacinto [n]	7th
Caldwell [s]	10th	Haskell [c, o]	13th	Starr [s, o]	15th
Coryell	11th	Hill [c]	6th	Stonewall [c,o]	13th
Crosby [c]	19th	Jim Hogg [s]	15th	Webb [s]	15th
Delta	1st	Kent [o]	13th	Williamson [c]	10th
Dickens [c]	19th	King	13th		

[n] County is in highest quartile of Negro proportion of population.
[s] County is in highest quartile of Latin-American proportion of population.
[c] County has over 20,000 acres devoted to cotton production.
[o] County crude oil production is over 10,000 barrels per day.

TABLE 5.
Republican Areas of Persistent Strength in Presidential Elections:
Counties in Highest Quartile of Party Vote—1952, '56, '60, '64.

County	Cong. Dist.	County	Cong. Dist.	County	Cong. Dist.
Austin [g, x]	9th	Gillespie [g, x]	21st	Midland [m, o, x]	16th
Bandera [x]	21st	Gray [w, o, x]	18th	Ochiltree [w, o, x]	18th
Cooke [o, x]	13th	Hemphill	18th	Randall [w, x]	18th
Dallas [m, x]	5th	Kendall [g, x]	21st	Roberts	18th
DeWitt [g, x]	14th	Kerr [x]	21st	Tom Green [m]	21st
Ector [m, o]	16th	Lipscomb [w, x]	18th	Uvalde [x]	21st
Edwards [x]	21st	Menard [x]	21st	Washington [g, x]	10th

[m] County contains a metropolitan area.
[g] One of the "German" Counties.
[w] County has over 50,000 acres devoted to wheat production.
[o] County crude oil production is over 10,000 barrels per day.
[x] County in highest quartile of vote: Texas Regulars + Republicans, '44.

easier to explain than their otherwise persistent adherence to the party. The counties are largely rural and agricultural.[15] Perhaps their performance indicates an extension of the tradition of the rural South, in which Democratic loyalty seems to have suffered only as a result of issues involving race or religion.

Comparative Analysis of the Presidential Election with the Yarborough-Bush Senatorial Election and Congressional Elections. Space limitations preclude any but the most cursory analysis of this aspect of the election. Two incumbent Republican congressmen were defeated, Bruce Alger in the 5th district and Ed Foreman in the 16th, along with all other Republican candidates for Congress. A lone GOP candidate (from Midland) was elected to the legislature. Statistically, the figures on the congressional contests do not suggest that the Johnson "coattails" were essential to the victories of Earle Cabell, who defeated Alger, or to Richard White, who defeated Foreman. In each case the Democratic congressional candidate ran slightly ahead of the President. White's percentage of the two-party vote was 57.1, compared with 56.5 in the district for LBJ. Cabell received 56.8 to Johnson's 54.8 in the 5th district.

A more detailed examination of the Senate race may be in order because of the advantage Johnson enjoys when his margin of success is compared with that of the winning Democratic incumbent, Senator Ralph W. Yarborough. The latter won over Republican George Bush by 329,621 compared with Johnson's margin over Goldwater of 704,619. Yarborough's percentage of the two-party vote was 56.3 and Johnson's was 63.4. *Hypothesis*: Senator Yarborough's victory was due to the Johnson "coattails" in the sense that the sweeping victory of the latter was essential to the success of the former. The question obviously calls for speculation and no positive answer can be given. Undoubtedly, Johnson furnished valuable assistance to Yarborough by discouraging opposition to him in the primary.[16] The metropolitan presses reported that only White House pressure prevented former congressman Joe Kilgore from entering the lists against the senior Texas Senator. During the general election campaign, Johnson furnished other aid. A Johnson confidant, Ed Clark of Austin, raised funds for Yarborough among businessmen. The President endorsed Yarborough and appeared with him in the Houston area during the final days of the campaign. The friendship of Johnson and Yarborough was of comparatively recent origin, beginning with

LBJ's assumption of the presidency. Prior to that event the two had been rivals for patronage and Democratic Party control in Texas. Johnson had allied with the conservatives in the party prior to 1960, and Yarborough gained the leadership of the liberal Democrats with his election to the Senate in 1957.

Several arguments in favor of the "coattail" theory may be noted. Texas permits straight ticket voting on its ballot, and undoubtedly the popularity of the President encouraged voters to choose a Senator favorable to LBJ and his program. Many other voters no doubt came to the polls to vote for Johnson and voted the straight

TABLE 6
Two-Party Trends In Texas Metropolitan Cos.:
Presidential Voting, 1944-1964

Year	Democratic Percentage	Republican Percentage	Net Change in Republican %	Deviation from Repub. Texas %
1944†	69.5	17.2		+0.5
1948*	60.2	30.1	+12.9	+5.6
1952	43.5	56.5	+26.4	+3.3
1956	40.6	59.4	+ 2.9	+3.7
1960	48.0	52.0	− 7.4	+3.0
1964	61.1	38.9	−13.1	+2.3

† 1944: Texas Regulars received 13.3% in metropolitan Cos., compared with 11.8% in the State; the deviation is +1.5.

* 1948: States Rights Democrats received 9.7% in metropolitan Cos., compared with 9.2% in the State; the deviation is +0.5.

TABLE 7
The Trend Toward Metropolitanism: Metropolitan Vote As A
Percentage Of Total Texas Vote In Presidential Elections,
1944-1964

Year	Vote in 19 Metropolitan Cos.	Percentage Increase
1944	43.1	
1948	46.3	+3.2
1952	51.5	+5.2
1956	54.4	+2.9
1960	57.2†	+2.8
1964	58.8*	+1.6

† 1960 population in the 19 metro counties — 58.2 per cent.

* 1964 population, based on estimate of the Texas Research League, 60.6 per cent.

TABLE 8
Two-Party Trend In Texas Non-Metropolitan Cos.:
Presidential Voting, 1944-1964

Year	Democratic Percentage	Republican Percentage	Net Change in Republican %	Deviation from Repub. Texas %
1944†	73.0	16.3		−0.4
1948*	71.6	19.6	+ 3.3	−4.9
1952	50.3	49.7	+30.1	−3.5
1956	48.7	51.3	+ 1.6	−4.4
1960	55.1	44.9	− 6.4	−4.1
1964	66.7	33.3	−11.6	−3.0

† 1944: Texas Regulars reecived 10.7% in non-metropolitan areas, compared with 11.8% in the State; the deviation is −1.1.

* 1948: States Rights Democrats received 8.7% in non-metropolitan areas, compared with 9.2% in the State; the deviation is −0.5.

ticket. Statistically, Yarborough received 199,227 fewer votes than LBJ. His foe, Bush, received 175,711 more votes than Goldwater.[17] Yarborough trailed Johnson in 250 of the 254 counties, and Bush ran ahead of Goldwater in 252 counties. Bush polled the largest popular vote ever accorded a Republican in Texas. Only Bowie County showed both a Yarborough advantage over Johnson and a Goldwater margin over Bush. The discrepancies between the Johnson and Yarborough votes were fairly uniform throughout the state, except in East Texas where the Johnson margin was narrow.

Yet Yarborough's victory was a comfortable one. He lost only 34 counties, virtually all of them in traditional Republican territory. Over the years he has shown tenacious support. Although Bush was a physically attractive candidate of the young executive type, he had never been a candidate for state office prior to 1964, and Texas has never elected a United States Senator who had no previous state-wide electoral experience. Bush Forces spent vast sums to combat the better-known incumbent.[18]

Some insight may be gained by a comparison of the Yarborough-Bush contest with the Tower-Blakley run-off election to choose a Senator in 1961 and to the Connally-Cox election of a Governor in 1962. The image of Yarborough as a weak candidate is refuted, if such a comparison is a useful measure, because Yarborough ran 2.1 per cent ahead of Connally and 6.9 per cent ahead of Blakley,[19] the Democratic candidates in these recent elections. Yarborough's advantage over Connally in the comparison is not great but it is consistent, even in a majority of the cities. The comparison suggests that Yarborough, like Connally, enjoyed "normal" Democratic support.

Metropolitan Republicanism. A conspicuous element of the "Eisenhower Republicanism" of 1952, 1956, and possibly 1960, was the presidential Republicanism of a number of cities in the hitherto "solid South." Nowhere was this trend more evident than in Texas. *Hypothesis:* The "backbone," or major element of Texas presidential Republicanism, is the metropolitan vote. To test this hypothesis, it must be shown that the metropolitan areas are significantly more Republican than the balance of the state and that the vote of the metropolitan areas is quantitatively significant. These demonstrations are achieved for the nineteen counties which include "metropolitan areas."[20] Table 5 lists the strongly Republican counties and Table 6 records the metropolitan percentages of the two-party votes. The latter table reveals that in each of the six most recent presidential elections Republican strength in these cities has exceeded that of the state. Table 6 shows that Republican strength in the metropolitan areas increased from 1944 to 1956. Since 1956 it has declined, suggesting that increased city strength has been an important factor in recent Democratic success. Table 7 records the metropolitan vote as a percentage of the total state vote, and shows that a majority of Texas presidential votes has been cast in the nineteen metro counties since 1952.

Table 8 records the two-party vote for non-metro areas, and it shows that here, too, Republican support increased from 1944 to 1956 and has since declined. Since the table is the reciprocal of Table 6, the Republican vote in the non-metro areas is consistently less than the state average, as well as the metro average. Yet the table makes it clear that Republican support in these non-metro areas has been an important factor in the recent strength of the party, although only once—in 1956—did the Republicans win a majority of votes in the areas outside the metro group.

The metro counties varied widely in the extent of their swing to Johnson. Tarrant County (Fort Worth) showed the largest swing, 18.3 per cent, followed by Dallas with a change of 17.5 per cent. It was in Fort Worth that Senator Goldwater uttered his tactless remarks about the TFX contract, awarded to a local firm. Fort Worth is also the home of Governor John Connally, a close and long-time friend of the President. The Dallas performance is in some ways the more startling. In 1960 Dallas County gave Nixon his largest voting percentage (62.7) of any major metropolitan area in the United States. The reversal of form, evident in the 1964 returns, owes something perhaps to sentiment resulting from the assassination of President Kennedy in the city, but organizational factors were a more tangible consideration. For once, the Dallas Democrats were vigorous in organizational and publicity efforts at the precinct level. For once the outspoken *Dallas Morning News* did not beat its drums for Republican candidates. For once, some, although not all, of the Dallas business "establishment" were active in behalf of a Democratic presidential aspirant.

At the lowest end of the list in terms of pro-Democratic change stand Jefferson (Beaumont), Ector (Odessa), Webb (Laredo), Smith (Tyler), and Midland Counties. It is perhaps significant that all of these counties except Webb are in the peripheral areas whose behavior was explained earlier in the light of a heartland theory. Three of them—Ector, Smith, and Midland—are counted among the traditional citadels of Texas Republicanism.

Harris (Houston) and Bexar (San Antonio) Counties are in the middle range of the list in terms of pro-Democratic change. Harris is Texas' most populous county, and in recent years it has been moderately Republican. Harris County produced small Republican majorities in two of the three Eisenhower-Nixon elections. Democratic forces in Harris, liberal-labor-Negro, have been active, though often a minority. Bexar County is perhaps the best weather vane in the state. It has backed the winner in each recent presidential election. With a sizeable Latin minority allied with Negro and other liberal forces and well organized, the San Antonio Democrats have vied with well organized Republicans who include a majority of the Anglo-Saxon component of the population. Congressman Henry B. Gonzalez, the first of Latin origin to win major office in modern Texas, has become the leading political figure of the county because of his ability to pile up huge victories in Latin and Negro precincts and to cut down his losses in Anglo precincts.

Obviously, not all of the nineteen metro counties were Republican during the Eisenhower-Nixon period. Two counties, Dallas and Midland, have been in the highest Republican quartile since 1948. Five counties, Ector, Harris, Potter, Smith, and Tom Green, have been in the highest quartile of Republicanism in four of the five presidential elections since 1948. Only one metro county, Webb (Laredo), has been in the highest Democratic quartile in four out of five of these elections. These counties have tended to be Democratic more often than not: Galveston, Jefferson (Beaumont), McLennan (Waco), Nueces (Corpus Christi), Travis (Austin), and Wichita (Wichita Falls). El Paso, like Bexar, has been a weather vane, and Lubbock and Taylor (Abilene) have been moderately Republican.

Roots of Republicanism. Tables 6 and 8 include data on third party movements in 1944 and 1948. The Texas Regulars (on the ballot in Texas in the 1944 presidential election) was a state-level protest by conservatives against the national Democrats. Unlike the southwide States Rights Democrats of 1948, the emphasis of the Regulars was on questions of economic policy rather than race.[21] *Hypothesis*: There is positive and significant correlation between areas of third party strength in 1944 and 1948 and areas of recent Republican strength. The answer with regard to the Dixiecrats is more clearly negative than in the case of the Regulars. Both third party groups ran more strongly in the cities than in the country, but the Regulars were stronger in both areas. Five counties in the highest quartile of Dixiecrat support have been regularly in the highest quartile of Republican strength. Eleven counties from the highest quartile of Regular voting have been consistently in the highest Republican quartile. Most significantly perhaps, seventeen of the counties among the Republican stalwarts (see Table 5) were in the highest quartile of anti-Democratic support (Regulars plus Republicans) in 1944.

Another locus of Republicanism in Texas is the "German counties" (see Table 9) about which V. O. Key said:

> During the (Civil) War they found themselves out of sympathy with their neighbors who would destroy the union to preserve slavery. The Germans were not slaveholders: they were liberals and revolutionists who took their American democracy literally. . . . Their Republicanism persists and some of these counties had a hand in the election of Texas' lone Republican Congressman (of the 1920s). . . .[22]

The sharp decline of Republican sentiment in the 1964 election may be partly explained by the proximity of the German counties to the LBJ Ranch.

A Note on Voter Turnout. Texas law provides for three classes of voters. Persons who qualify to vote by paying a poll tax are required to present a poll tax receipt when they appear to vote.

TABLE 9

Locus of Republicanism In Presidential Elections: The German Counties of Texas, 1944-1964 (Republican % of Two-Party Vote)

County	1944	1948	1952	1956	1960	1964
Austin	19.5r	44.1*	67.2*	67.3*	53.4*	39.5*
Comal	67.7*	57.1*	73.0*	74.9*	62.6*	37.9
DeWitt	44.9*	44.4*	67.8*	70.3*	55.1*	41.0*
Fayette	26.8*	33.0*	62.4*	61.0*	39.0	35.9
Gillespie	82.6*	80.4*	92.5*	92.8*	76.7*	42.8*
Guadalupe	58.9*	51.3*	65.4*	67.2*	54.0*	37.4
Kendall	76.0*	67.7*	82.8*	81.7*	73.8*	55.3*
Lee	35.3*	22.0	48.7	53.1	43.4	32.9
Medina	47.5*	42.5*	63.5*	63.8*	46.6	31.7
Washington	13.3r	50.9*	72.2*	76.1*	58.4*	40.7*

* The asterisk indicates that the county was in the highest quartile of Republican support. r Indicates heavy vote for the Texas Regulars in 1944.

S. S. McKay, *Texas Politics, 1906-1944* (Lubbock: Texas Tech Press: 1952) is the most intensive treatment of the "German counties." The ten counties in the table are those which McKay identifies. The *Texas Almanac, 1956-'57*, notes German settlements in nine of these counties before the Civil War, but the names of settlements, Westhoff, Lindeman, and Nordheim in DeWitt Co. (the tenth) suggest the merits of its inclusion. Clifton McCleskey, *The Government and Politics of Texas* (Boston: Little, Brown: 1963), pp. 83-84, identifies fifteen "German counties" excluding Fayette and Medina of those above and adding Calhoun, Colorado, Goliad, Kerr, Lavaca, Mason, and Victoria. V. O. Key, *Southern Politics*, pp. 274-276, suggests "The German counties of today are not readily identifiable, for there is no way to determine *the exact proportions of the population of German origin*."

Persons voting for the first time and persons over sixty years of age are not required to pay the poll tax in order to vote, but they are required to present a poll tax exemption certificate at the polls, if they live in cities of ten thousand population or more. Persons over sixty who live in smaller cities or rural areas are not required to present a certificate in order to vote.[23] As a consequence of the ratification of the 24th amendment to the U.S. Constitution, a fourth class of Texas voters was created—persons who may vote in federal elections *only*, without paying a poll tax. Statistics on qualified voters are obviously incomplete, because no records are available of persons over sixty who live in small cities or rural areas. Where the voting polls are complete the actual vote total may exceed the number of voters listed as qualified. In the 1964 election for President this phenomenon occurred in 37 counties. In 59 other counties the actual vote exceeded ninety per cent of the number listed as "qualified."

In order to be meaningful, measurements of voter turnout in Texas should avoid comparison with the number listed as "qualified," since the latter is incomplete. In the following analysis actual turnout is figured as a percentage of persons of voting age. *Hypothesis*: Texas voter turnout compares unfavorably with national voter turnout (slightly above sixty per cent of voting age population in 1960 and 1964).

Actual voter turnout in Texas was 42.1 per cent of the voting age population in the presidential election of 1960, and 43.9 per cent in the same election of 1964.[24] The bite of these figures—more than fifteen per cent below the national average—is emphasized by the fact that these two elections occasioned the largest turnout in Texas history.

Historically, low voter turnout in the South has been considered a product of (a) the absence of two-party competition and (b) the apathy of ethnic minorities, or in some cases the intimidation of members of these minorities. But Texas has been a two-party state, at least on the level of presidential and senatorial elections, and intimidation of ethnic minorities has not been evident in recent years. Can low voter turnout in the state be attributed to apathy among the ethnic minorities, Negroes and Latin Americans? *Hypothesis*: Voter turnout by congressional districts has high positive correlation with Anglo population.[25] Voter turnout by congressional districts has high negative correlation with Negro and Latin population.

For 1960 turnout in the presidential election, the mean is 41.7 per cent and the standard deviation is 3.62. For 1964 the mean is 43.5 per cent and the standard deviation is 3.83. For Anglo population the mean is 73.9 per cent and the standard deviation is 13.7. For 1960 the Pearson coefficient of correlation is +.564. The 1964 Pearson coefficient of correlation is +.513. The Pearson coefficient of correlation for voter turnout and Negro population is, for 1960, +.067, and for 1964, +.342. The Pearson coefficient for turnout and Latin population (Spanish surnames) is, for 1960, —.430, and for 1964, —.483.[26]

This evidence indicates that two-thirds of the hypothesis is valid. Anglo population correlates with turnout in a highly positive manner and Latin population has a strongly negative correlation with turnout. For Negro population, however, there is a small positive correlation in 1960 and a somewhat larger positive correlation in 1964. The figures alone do not *prove* that Latins are apathetic in contrast to Negroes, but the fact is strongly suggested.

Other evidence tends to verify the conclusions suggested by the Pearson coefficients. Negroes, qualified for voting in Texas, increased from 226,818 in 1960 to 375,000 in 1964. The latter figure represents 57.7 per cent of the voting age population of Texas Negroes. The increase is 65.3 per cent![27] The estimate of actual Negro vote in 1964 is 308,400. While Latin population in Texas is almost two and one-half per cent larger than Negro population, the *Texas Observer* estimated that Negro vote in the state exceeded Latin vote by some 65,000! This study estimates that the ratio of "qualified" Negro voters to the voting age population of Negroes is slightly lower than the equivalent figure (percentage) for Anglos. It is estimated that the ratio of actual voters to "qualified" persons was about the same for Negroes and Anglos in 1964. Yet voter turnout among all ethnic groups is low compared with the national average.

It seems logical to conclude from these figures that Negroes in Texas vote in equivalent or larger proportions than do Anglos of comparable income and educational levels. Over-all Anglo income and educational levels are considerably higher than those of Negroes, and Anglo voter turnout is slightly higher as a percentage of voting age population.

Lagging voter participation among Latins in Texas may be explained as a consequence of several factors. Of 241,000 resident aliens in the state, 204,000 are Mexican nationals. According to census figures for 1960, 38 per cent of the Latins aged fourteen and above, have five years schooling or less. The equivalent Negro percentage is 19 per cent and the figure for Anglos is 5 per cent. Of the three ethnic groups median income per family is lowest among Latins. Perhaps cultural isolation also plays a part in the voter apathy of the group.

Conclusions. A decade and a half prior to the 1964 presidential election, V. O. Key noted that Texas was an exception to the norm of Southern political preoccupation with the "issue" of the Negro. Key discerned in Texas "a politics of economics." While an impressionistic interpretation of Texas politics strongly suggests that the characterization by V. O. Key was still valid in 1964, the aims of this study have precluded a direct examination of the Key thesis. Rather the paper has focused on other aspects of Texas political phenomena: ethnic and regional voting tendencies and the cleavage of metropolitan and rural voters. Although

East Texas voting in 1964 was influenced to a minor degree by "white backlash," this effect contrasted with remarkable sharpness to its powerful impact upon adjacent states of the old South. While the Texas cities remained relatively more Republican than the surrounding country in 1964, they contributed to the conspicuous resurgence of Democratic strength which was manifested so clearly in the victory of President Johnson and almost the entire state Democratic ticket. Negro voters, and to a much less extent, Latin-American voters, both normally a part of the Democratic coalition, contributed to the resurgence by means of increased participation and by the solidity of their support of President Johnson. The candidacy of a Texas President augmented the already-evident tendency of the Texas heartland to support the Democrats, the pheripheral districts of East and West Texas remained relatively more favorable to the Republicans, although even here Democratic strength increased.

FOOTNOTES

[1] *Southern Politics In State and Nation* (New York: Alfred A. Knopf: 1949), p. 255.

[2] Viz.: the Shivers-Ralph Yarborough primary in '54, the Daniel-Yarborough run-off in '56, the Connally-Don Yarborough run-off in '62. Closest of all have been senatorial contests: the O'Daniel-Johnson race of '41, the O'Daniel-Allred primary of '42, the Johnson-Stevenson run-off in '48.

[3] Texas Congressman Bruce Alger went to the 1960 Republican National Convention pledged to support Richard M. Nixon for the presidential nomination. After Nixon compromised his differences with liberal New York Governor Nelson Rockefeller, Alger sought to nominate Senator Barry Goldwater to be presidential standard-bearer. But the Arizona Senator, noting his own commitment to Nixon, declined to have his name considered. He urged his fellow conservatives to look to the future and to organize, if they hoped to influence party policy. In a sense the Goldwater drive for the 1964 nomination began when he declined to offer as a candidate in 1960.

Organized activity in behalf of the Arizonan was initiated at a secret meeting held in Chicago on December 2, 1962. Texas Republican Chairman Peter O'Donnell, Jr. headed the national Goldwater drive, and he received strong support from John Tower, who had won the special election in 1961 to fill the senatorial chair formerly occupied by Lyndon B. Johnson. Even before the Chicago meeting, "Goldwater in '64" stickers had begun to appear on automobiles in various parts of the country. The stickers were exceptionally numerous in North Dallas, Texas.

[4] For an indication of "the fallacy of ecological correlation," see W. S. Robinson, "Ecological Correlation and the Behavior of Individuals," *American Sociological Review,* vol. XV (1950), pp. 351-57. On the other hand, ecological correlation does have valid uses, if care is taken to prevent variables from being obscured: See Leo A. Goodman, "Ecological Regression and Behavior of Individuals," *American Sociological Review,* vol. XVIII (1953), pp. 663-64. See also Leo A. Goodman, "Some Alternatives to Ecological Correlation," *American Journal of Sociology,* vol. 64 (May 1959), pp. 610-25.

In some cases, correlations of coefficients are *only suggestive* of certain relationships. In the present study, for instance, the positive correlation between the size of the Latin-American population proportion in a congressional district and the tendency of the district to support the Democrats *does not prove* that Latin-Americans vote Democratic, although they probably do. The findings prove only the hypothesis: that Democratic tendency varies directly with the Latin-American proportion of population by districts. To show empirically that Latin-Americans vote Democratic, we should have to rely on interviews with these voters, or a representative sampling of them. But this is beyond the resources of the researcher in the present study.

In the absence of more expensive scientific methods, correlations serve several useful purposes:

(a) They offer the advantage of precision in stating a problem and in presenting tentative findings.

(b) Even if the finding is expressed as a coarse measurement, as in the example cited above, it may be the best, or only, measurement available.

(c) The method may produce clues which are valuable in suggesting the direction and content of further investigation.

(d) A by-product of correlational analysis may be the discovery of unexpected insights.

[5] The outcome of a presidential preference primary in Texas probably disappointed the Goldwaterites. Only 139,323 votes were cast, according to the Texas Election Bureau, with Goldwater receiving 74.7 per cent. Other names on the ballot, Governor Nelson Rockefeller, Senator Margaret Chase Smith, and Harold Stassen, received 11.8 per cent. Write-in votes were cast for Henry Cabot Lodge and Richard Nixon with Lodge getting 8.8 per cent, making him the second most popular candidate.

[6] Texans, like Americans elsewhere, saw much of the campaign on television. Goldwater use of the medium seemed essentially defensive. His spots and programs were largely designed to reassure the voters that he was not trigger happy, that he did not plan to abolish social security, that he was a calm and reasonable man.

In September the Democrats used and then abandoned the infamous ad showing a child plucking a daisy. The child said that a bad man named Goldwater wanted to blow up the world. A more effective Democratic ad recounted pre-nomination anti-Goldwater statements by Republicans Romney, Scranton, and Rockefeller. Probably the most effective Democratic ad depicted the "awful loneliness of the Presidency" and noted that most of our Presidents have been responsible men. It ended with the words, "Vote for President Johnson on November 3rd. The stakes are too high for you to stay at home."

Both parties, and the Democrats in particular, seemed to fear voter apathy. A non-partisan t-v spot repeated the slogan: "Vote and the choice is yours. Don't vote and the choice is theirs."

[7] The Texas poll, a sampling by Belden Associates of Dallas which ran in several state newspapers, showed President Johnson far in the lead throughout the campaign. The Belden poll has proven badly wrong in some recent state elections, but has a better record in reporting presidential elections. In private polls purchased by his foes, Senator Yarborough enjoyed a comfortable lead until near the end of the campaign. Although Yarborough actually won handily, a final, adverse poll probably contributed to the report that he owed his election over Republican George Bush to the Presidential coattails of LBJ.

[8] The exceptions are Franklin and Van Zandt. Negro population percentages in the districts are 26.6, 21.6, and 24.7 respectively.

[9] A separate section of the paper is devoted to voter turnout, including a discussion of Negro voting. See pp. 47-51.

[10] The other three are Starr (15th district) Glasscock (16th), and Martin (19th).

[11] See L. L. Thurstone, *The Fundamental of Statistics* (New York: MacMillan Company: 1925) pp. 100-104, 205-223.

[12] For purposes of analysis, the Democratic vote in the 8th district is estimated at 65.6 per cent and for the 22nd district at 51.6 per cent. These estimates are necessary because the official returns do not include the separate figures for the two districts within Harris County. Other district figures are found in Table 3, above.

[13] Figures on Negro population and Spanish surnames are taken from the U.S. Bureau of the Census, *Congressional District Data Book* (Washington, D.C.: U.S. Gov. Printing Office: 1962), pp. 400, 492.

[14] In only three Texas congressional districts are the combined Negro and Latin population less than fourteen per cent: the 18th—7.7; the 13th—8.1; the 17th—8.4. The 13th district has been consistently Democratic; the 17th was strongly Democratic

in 1964, although not in the Eisenhower-Nixon elections; the 18th has been one of the stronger Republican areas.

[15] In this study efforts to correlate certain socio-economic data with voting tendencies has failed to demonstrate any significant relationships.

Cattle raising was rejected as a measure because it is too widely practiced in Texas to permit useful differentiation. Little positive correlation was found between the 77 counties heavily devoted to cotton (20,000 acres or more) and Democratic voting, although the correlation of cotton counties and Republicanism is strongly negative: —.5625.

Regarding correlation between counties which lead in production of crude oil (over 10,000 barrels per day) and party preferences, the figures are not statistically significant and may be accounted for by the chance factor alone. A few counties with high production of crude oil are among the regular Democratic and Republican stalwarts (see Tables 4 and 5).

Thirteen of the twenty Texas counties, in which wheat production exceeds fifty thousand acres, are in the highest quartile of Republican counties for 1964. Yet the correlation seems more geographical than occupational. All of the Republican wheat counties are in the upper Panhandle, adjacent to the Republicanism of the Oklahoma Panhandle and of western Kansas. Counties in the upper Texas Panhandle, in which wheat production is not high, have been as strongly Republican as the wheat counties in the region.

[16] Dallas radio executive Gordon McLendon ran and was defeated.

[17] A coattail theory based on discrepancies in the votes for two candidates on the same party ticket would lead to embarrassing complications. For instance, Governor John Connally led Johnson by two hundred thousand and Connally's opponent, Jack Crichton, trailed Goldwater by two hundred and fifty thousand.

[18] According to Yarborough, Bush outspent him in the ratio of three to one. Whatever the discrepancy, it was exceptionally evident in television exposure and billboard advertising.

[19] Blakley probably failed to poll the "normal" Democratic strength because his somewhat racist campaign alienated liberal voters. The *Texas Observer*, organ of Democratic liberals, urged its readers to "go fishing."

[20] According to U. S. Census definition (1960), 29 Texas counties are included in Standard Metropolitan Statistical Areas. In this analysis, however, Archer, Bowie, Cameron, Collin, Denton, Ellis, Johnson, Jones, Orange, and Randall Counties have been excluded because, during most of the time period studied, these counties were too small and too distant from "core" cities in the metro areas to be considered comparable for purposes of political analysis.

[21] Key, *Southern Politics*, p. 256, says: "The Texas Regulars were more concerned about economics than race, but they adopted a resolution condemning Supreme Court decisions in the white-primary cases and alleged efforts to break down segregation."

[22] *Southern Politics*, pp. 275-276.

[23] *Tex. Sess. Laws*, 58th Leg., Reg. Sess., ch. 424, § 28, p. 1017. See also *Opinions*, *Atty. Gen.*, 2434 (1940).

[24] Estimated population growth from 1960 to 1964 is based on a projection by the Texas Research League. The League estimated that 1965 Texas population would be 10,650,000 with all gain occurring in the 29 counties included in the U. S. Census Bureau listing of Standard Metropolitan Statistical Areas. 1964 population is computed at 4/5 of this five year growth. Voting age population (1960 basis) is 57.3 per cent of total population. See *Texas Almanac, 1964-1965*, p. 112.

[25] To facilitate statistical precision, the term "Anglo," as used herein, denotes total population for the political unit, less Negroes and persons with Spanish surnames.

[26] Percentage means and standard deviations for Negro and Latin populations by congressional districts are found on pp. 27-28.

[27] These data were obtained from the Southern Regional Council, Atlanta, Georgia. The Council estimated the Negro vote as slightly higher than the figures used here.

The 1964 Presidential Election in Oklahoma

JOHN W. WOOD*

University of Oklahoma

The comment that "Oklahoma has been a predominantly one-party, Democratic state since statehood was achieved in 1907,"[1] holds considerable validity. Oklahoma voters first participated in a presidential election in 1908. Reversing territorial history, dominated by Republican governors, and territorial representatives to Congress, the voters cast 48.1% of the vote for Democrat William Jennings Bryan as compared to 43.4% for Republican William Howard Taft, winner of the national election. In ten of the fifteen presidential elections since statehood Oklahoma voters have cast a plurality or majority of the vote for Democratic presidential candidates (Table 1).

That one-third of all presidential elections since 1908 in Oklahoma have been won by Republican presidential contenders is misleading as an indication of the extent of party competition within *state* politics. Ranney and Kendall classify Oklahoma as a "modified one-party" state in their classification of state party systems based on presidential, senatorial and gubernatorial elections from 1914 to 1954.[2] After surveying various methods used for classification of state party systems, the *Oklahoma Votes, 1907-1962* study agrees with the "modified one-party" classification. A more competitive party system than normally assumed exists in Oklahoma if the Democratic percentage of the total vote in elections for major offices is used as the index for party competition (Table 2).

---

* The author wishes to acknowledge the use of materials by Oliver Benson, Harry Holloway, George Mauer, Joseph Pray, and Wayne Young, in *Oklahoma Votes, 1907-1962*, Bureau of Government Research, University of Oklahoma, Norman, 1964. Voting data in *Oklahoma Votes, 1907-1962*, are derived from the Oklahoma Election Board and provides the most reliable and complete compilation of election results of Oklahoma elections. Data on the 1964 elections are from *State of Oklahoma Election Results and Statistics, 1964*, compiled by Frank Reneau, Secretary, State Election Board, Oklahoma City, Oklahoma.

Also, I wish to acknowledge the assistance of students in Government 440—Seminar in Political Behavior. They have helped to bring the election data up to date for 1964.

Table 1

Percent of Popular Vote Received by Presidential Candidates in Oklahoma, 1908-1964

	1948	1952	1956	1960	1964
Truman	62.7				
Dewey	37.2				
Stevenson		45.4	44.8		
Eisenhower		54.5	55.1		
Kennedy				40.9	
Nixon				59.0	
Johnson					55.75
Goldwater					44.25

	1928	1932	1936	1940	1944
Smith	35.4				
Hoover	63.7	26.7			
Roosevelt		73.2	66.8	57.4	55.5
Langdon			32.6		
Wilkie				42.2	
Dewey					44.2
Other	.8		.4	.3	.2

	1908	1912	1916	1920	1924
Bryan	48.1				
Wilson		46.9	50.6		
Taft	43.4	35.7			
Hughes			32.2		
Cox				44.5	
Harding				50.2	
Davis					48.4
Coolidge					42.7
Other	8.4	17.2	16.0	5.3	8.7

Source: *Oklahoma Votes, 1907-1962*, pp. 62-68, updated for 1964 presidential election.

TABLE 2
MAJOR RACES IN STATEHOOD HISTORY AND RECENT PERIODS:
DEMOCRATIC PERCENTAGE OF THE TOTAL VOTE

Type of Election	Per Cent	Statehood History	Per Cent	Recent Contests
Gubernatorial	54.9	(1907-1962)	55.4	(1942-1962)
Presidential	51.8	(1908-1964)	46.7	(1952-1964)
Senatorial	55.5	(1912-1964)	55.1	(1948-1964)

Source: *Oklahoma Votes, 1907-1962*, p. 50, updated for the 1964 presidential and senate elections.

A REINSTATING ELECTION

The predominantly one-party Democratic or "modified one-party" character of Oklahoma's party system appeared to be changing after Richard M. Nixon maintained the state in the Republican column for a third successive presidential election in 1960. Whether or not this may be substantiated on a long range basis remains indecisive. After the 1964 presidential election in which President Lyndon Johnson polled 519,834 votes or 55.75% of the total vote in Oklahoma, it appears that an interruption has resulted in the shift toward a more competitive two-party system.

Converse, Campbell, Miller and Stokes of the University of Michigan Survey Research Center extend their nomenclature after analysis of the 1960 presidential election to include the term "reinstating"—an election "in which the party enjoying a majority of party identifiers returns to power."[3] The 1964 presidential election in Oklahoma might be viewed as a "reinstating" election for the Democratic Party if the terminology derived by Converse, and Associates of "deviating," "maintaining," and "reinstating" is applied on a more limited single state basis.

Voting preferences in Oklahoma throughout history have favored the Democratic Party in contests for presidential, senatorial, gubernatorial, and lesser state offices. The normal expectation in gubernatorial and senatorial elections is a 55/45 division favoring the Democratic Party. In presidential elections since statehood a 52/48 division with a Democratic Party advantage is evident (Table 2). Expectation of the Republican Party to win substantial numbers of statewide elections with some degree of frequency is limited, as indicated by the Republican victories in

TABLE 3

VOTER REGISTRATION IN OKLAHOMA, 1964-1965

	January, 1964	November, 1964	Percentage Two Party Registration	Increase Over January, 1964	Percentage Of Total Increase	February, 1965	Percentage Two Party Registration
Democratic	986,470	1,058,465	81%	71,995	83%	953,243	80%
Republican	233,238	248,458	19%	15,220	17%	231,458	20%
Independent	4,702	5,941				4,941	
Total Registration	1,224,410	1,311,864	100%	87,212	100%	1,189,026	100%

Source: Secretary, State Election Board.

TABLE 4

CROSS-OVER VOTE—1964 GENERAL ELECTION FOR U.S. SENATE

	May Primary	November General Election	Gain or Loss
Republican	126,925	445,392	+218,467
Democratic	591,326	466,782	−124,544
Total	718,251	912,174	

five of fifteen presidential elections, electing three U.S. Senators, and only one governor since 1908.

Party identification as indicated by voter registration works to the advantage of the Democratic Party as does the closed primary election. Before the 1964 presidential election the Democrats had 81% of the major party registration (Table 3). The Republican victories in presidential elections (1952-1960), concerted efforts on the part of Republican party workers, and the change-over of Bud Wilkinson to the Republican party in order to file as a candidate in the May primaries, had little impact on the tendency of electors to register as Democrats (Table 3). The Republican primary election, except for offices at the top of the ticket, has for the most part remained a deserted one. Bud Wilkinson aptly stated the dilemma of a Republican in Oklahoma at the time he changed his party registration:[4]

> I was a registered Republican before moving to Oklahoma 18 years ago. Mary (Wilkinson's wife) and I registered as Democrats because, at that time, there was little opportunity for a Republican to cast an effective vote in primary elections.

The overwhelming tendency for Republican identifiers to register as Democrats has led to a large number of ideological Republicans, officially registered as Democrats, who cross-over and vote for Republican candidates in the general election. To illustrate, Bud Wilkinson received 218,467 votes more in the November general election (1964) than were cast for Republican senatorial candidates in the May primary (Table 4).

RECENT REPUBLICAN PARTY STRENGTH

Samuel Lubell's thesis that the Democratic Party is the nation's majority in the post-1932 period appears to be valid for Oklahoma as for the nation.[5] Dwight D. Eisenhower, popular World War II military hero, took the Oklahoma voters away from their predominant Democratic preference in 1952, with 54.5% of the popular vote, and increased his majority slightly to 55.1% in 1956. In 1960, 59.0% of the vote went for Richard M. Nixon. Therefore the 1952-1962 decade of Oklahoma politics must be viewed as a "temporary deviation" from dominant Democratic Party control such as that which occurred in 1920-1928. Paradoxically, the outer limits of both periods of "temporary deviation" were ended with presidential elections (1928 and 1960) in which the Democratic

Party presented a Catholic as its nominee. Whenever the national Democratic Party has found it advantageous to nominate a Catholic for their candidate, the Oklahoma Democrats have had extreme difficulty in maintaining the party allegiance of the voters.

Oklahoma election results on occasions have been notorious for their sporadic "flip-flops" in presidential elections—shifting the state from substantial or even landslide victories for the Republican Party, as in 1928, to the Democratic column four years later in 1932. A similar development in 1960 and 1964 adds credence to the thesis of "no-party" analysis, or that of the "end of ideology" as applied to the state's voters.[6] This suggests that party identification in Oklahoma—Democratic Party identification—is becoming less important in voter preferences.

Election of Henry Bellmon as the state's first Republican governor in 1962 was in the wake of a deep division within Democratic Party ranks after an especially bitter run-off primary election between W. P. "Bill" Atkinson and former Governor Raymond Gary. Although Atkinson won the run-off election (so close it led to a recount) his victory was at the expense of a disunited party which opened the way for the election of Bellmon in the November general election. Bellmon polled 55.3% of the total vote, 75,000 more votes than his Democratic opponent.

Professor Harry Holloway of the University of Oklahoma has analyzed the Democratic Party split which occurred in the 1962 election with considerable precision.[7] After the run-off primary election former Governor Raymond Gary refused to endorse his opponent and failed to heal party wounds. Gary took the position that he would vote the Democratic ticket, but opposed Atkinson's proposal for an increase in the sales tax and took offense at his "urban outlook and associations." Professor Holloway found a "correlation between the Bellmon vote and Gary strength" sufficient to indicate that Democratic Party disunity was a major cause, politically, for Atkinson's defeat, although the sales tax increase issue, impact of urbanization on the vote, opposition to Atkinson in the metropolitan press, and candidate personalities played important roles.

PARTY COMPETITION—1964 PRESIDENTIAL ELECTION

Despite Lyndon Johnson's 1964 presidential victory in Oklahoma with its "reinstating" effect, strong argument exists that Oklahoma has achieved a more competitive party system, if not two-party competition, in gubernatorial, senatorial and presidential elections. The 55.7% margin of the vote received by Johnson in 1964 lagged 5.7% behind his 61.4% margin of the total two-party vote nationwide. Senator Barry Goldwater, Republican candidate, polled 44.25% of the vote in Oklahoma, running considerably ahead of his national average—attached to the "tear-away shirt tails" of Bud Wilkinson, nearly victorious, but defeated Republican candidate for the U.S. Senate.

The margin of victory for the Democratic candidate in 1964 did not equal the resounding landslides for Franklin D. Roosevelt in 1932 and 1936, nor reach the 62.7% cast for Harry S. Truman in 1948 (Table 1). Lyndon Johnson ranks third in the popularity list for Democratic presidential candidates in state history, running well behind the support given Franklin D. Roosevelt and Harry S. Truman. The margin of difference between the Truman vote in 1948 and Johnson vote in 1964, slightly under 7%, provides a superficial measurement that the state is less Democratic than before the Republican victories in the 1950's and in 1960.

Why did the Johnson percentage margin of victory in Oklahoma fall behind his national average in 1964? Before the last election the Democratic percentage of the state's popular vote had fallen below the national average of the Party only in the elections of 1928 and 1960 where the Catholic religious issue played a prominant role. In 1960 the Democratic percentage in Oklahoma decreased 3.9% below the 1956 percentage which allowed the Republican Party to pick up additional voters, presumably on the religious issue (Table 5).

TABLE 5

DEVIATION PERCENTAGE—OKLAHOMA DEMOCRATIC VOTE FROM U.S. DEMOCRATIC VOTE, 1952-1964

Presidential Election	U.S. Democratic Vote %	Oklahoma Democratic Vote %	Deviation Percentage
1952	44.6	45.2	1.4
1956	42.2	44.8	2.6
1960	50.1	40.9	—9.2
1964	61.4	55.7	—5.7

Source: *Oklahoma Votes, 1907-1962*, pp. 67-68, updated for 1964 presidential election.

The 55.75% margin of the vote polled by Lyndon Johnson seems to be a much larger increase in Democratic strength if it is noted that he had to regain the loss in party vote due to the Kennedy defeat in Oklahoma. The Democratic percentage was increased by 14.8% over 1960; still the percentage was 5.7% below the national average. Again this may suggest a net gain in Republican Party strength long range in nature. It is yet too soon to substantiate an argument that the "temporary deviations" of the 1952-1962 era elevate the Republican Party to a permanently competitive position.

ELECTORAL FOUNDATIONS IN OKLAHOMA

The population influx into Oklahoma in the 1890's and early in this century resulted in the newcomers transplanting their partisan feelings. V. O. Key cites Oklahoma as an example of this occurrence in *American State Politics*.[8] Along with economic divisions on an agricultural base, development of natural resources, recent trends toward urbanization, increasing number of aged population, and those on welfare, the early migrations set the basic pattern for Oklahoma politics. Ewing and Benson in the 1952 study of presidential nominating politics summarize succinctly the meaning of early settlement patterns in the state's politics:[9]

> The Northern tier of counties has been consistently Republican since before statehood. The people settling in that strip of more than four hundred miles in length were largely from northern states in the union, especially from Kansas. On the other hand, the people near the Arkansas border on the east and Texas border on the south are overwhelmingly Democratic. The center of the state is a meeting ground of these two waves of migration and is an area of political contest, although the Democrats have enjoyed a fairly safe majority since statehood.

Patterns of settlement as related to politics are reinforced on an economic base. The north central and northwestern counties are devoted to wheat as an agricultural product, as opposed to the south and southwestern counties and their cotton economy. The northern counties toward the east, Tulsa and Washington, have become the headquarters of the petroleum industry. The southeastern counties are low in per capita income and usually high on percentage of population over 65 and numbers of welfare recipients.

Population Trends

Oklahoma's 1960 population was 2,328,284, an increase over 1950 of 94,933. Population increases between 1950 and 1960 were evident in only thirteen counties, and of significant proportions in only six counties, as 64 counties lost population of about 200,000. The population has moved from the farm and into the cities— chiefly the major cities of Oklahoma City and Tulsa. Those counties which experienced population gains in 1960 included Cleveland and Oklahoma, which are adjoining, and together account for 43% of the total urban increase of 279,155. Tulsa and Washington counties account for 37% of the total increase, and the only remaining center of significant population growth is in the southwestern counties, Comanche and Jackson, with about 20% increase. Comanche County contains the city of Lawton and Ft. Sill Military Base. Population decline between 1950 and 1960 was considerable, 13% in 13 counties, including the Panhandle of the northwest. The most severe losses were in 15 counties of the southeast, a 20% loss.[10]

Urbanization and the Vote

What is the impact of urbanization on the development of Republican Party strength in Oklahoma? The 1952, 1956 and 1960 presidential election returns indicate a "neat linear correspondence of size of population and Republican vote" although this is broken by medium-sized counties in the 25,000-49,999 population group (Table 6).

TABLE 6
URBANIZATION AND REPUBLICAN VOTE

Population Group		Number of Counties	Average Per Cent Of Republican Vote Presidential	
			1952-56-60	1964
No. 1	100,000 up	2	61.5	51.3
No. 2	50,000-99,999	4	58.8	44.2
No. 3	25,000-49,999	19	49.4	38.3
No. 4	10,000-24,999	32	55.4	41.9
No. 5	Under 10,000	20	53.3	41.1

Source: *Oklahoma Votes, 1907-1962*, p. 13, updated for the 1964 presidential election.

The returns for the 1964 presidential election correlate almost
perfectly with the earlier findings in *Oklahoma Votes, 1907-1962*
(Table 6). The Republican vote in 1964 is lower in each county
population group, indicative of the fact that Barry Goldwater ran
poorly in relation to Eisenhower and Nixon regardless of the
population group of the county. The greatest difference is between the 1952, 1956, 1960 and the 1964 percentages in the
50,000-99,999 population group, a decline of 14.6%. The lowest
difference is in the 100,000 and up group, which includes only
Tulsa and Oklahoma counties, a decline of 10.2%. The average
decline for all population groups is 12.3%.

Although it is thought that the impact of urbanization has led
to some increase in Republican strength in recent elections, the
"size of county population (urbanization) does not appear to be
playing a critical role as yet in influencing the voting behavior of
the residents of various counties."[11] As Wayne Young demonstrates
in his analysis, a cause-effect relationship between the variables
of size of county and Republican vote is somewhat dubious.
Young's analysis of past voting records of counties shown in the
population groups (Table 6) concludes that "past voting records
of the residents of the various counties appears to be the critical
factor in understanding the voting behavior in these counties."[12]

A MAINTAINING ELECTION

The Democratic Party retained its dominant position without
loss of substantial strength in congressional and state legislative
races in Oklahoma in 1964 and in this context we may extend the
terminology of Converse and Associates to designate it a "maintaining" election. In this type of election "the pattern of partisan
attachments prevailing in the preceding period persists and is the
primary influence on forces governing the vote."[13] To discover
appreciable increase in Republican Party strength as a result of
the recent election depends primarily on the closely contested
election between Democrat Fred R. Harris and Republican Bud
Wilkinson for the two year unexpired term in the U.S. Senate left
vacant by the death of Robert S. Kerr.

The untimely death of Senator Kerr, early in 1963, brought the
resignation of Governor J. Howard Edmondson. Lt. Governor
George Nigh succeeded to the office left vacant. He subsequently
appointed Edmondson to the senate vacancy to serve until the
next regular general election, November, 1964.

Coattail Effect—Senate Election

President Lyndon Johnson with 55.75% of the total vote carried 62 Oklahoma counties in the 1964 presidential election. He lost only 15 of the 77 counties to Senator Barry Goldwater (Map A). Fred R. Harris, Democratic candidate for U.S. Senate, ran 21,390 votes ahead of his Republican opponent Bud Wilkinson to win the Senate election by a narrow margin, 51.1% of the total vote. Harris trailed 53,052 votes behind the presidential ticket headed by Lyndon Johnson. Without the "presidential coattails" Harris would have encountered extensive difficulty in defeating the former football coach of the University of Oklahoma.

Harris maintained strength in the strongly Democratic counties of southwest, south and southeast Oklahoma (Map B). In Cotton, Leflore and Sequoyah counties he ran slightly ahead of the presidential ticket. In the remaining 74 counties he trailed the presidential ticket. Johnson carried Oklahoma county, the crucial swing county which had been in the Republican column for the last three presidential elections. Harris ran 14,584 votes behind the president in Oklahoma county, which he lost, and 9,459 votes behind in Tulsa county. The two metropolitan counties accounted for more than half the deficit for the senatorial candidate. Except for the two metropolitan counties the incidence of ticket splitting was almost evenly distributed throughout the state in areas of Democratic presidential strength.

Bud Winkinson polled 32,727 votes more in the Senate race than Barry Goldwater received in the presidential election in Oklahoma. Goldwater carried 15 counties, all of which are normally found in the strongly Republican classification in presidential elections (based on 1952-1960). He carried nine of the 15 counties by a 55% margin or over, the remaining 6 by a 50-55% vote margin (Table 7; Map A). Goldwater lost 19 counties which are classified as strongly Republican as to distribution of party strength in presidential elections from 1952-1960.

The Goldwater-Miller ticket ran ahead of the Republican senatorial candidate in the three Panhandle counties (Beaver, Cimmaron and Texas) by a total of only 50 votes. In the 15 counties carried by Goldwater-Miller, Wilkinson ran ahead by a net total of 9,903 votes. In the 12 counties carried by Wilkinson and lost to Johnson-Humphrey by the Goldwater-Miller ticket, a 21,107 vote margin separated the senatorial candidate from the presidential ticket.

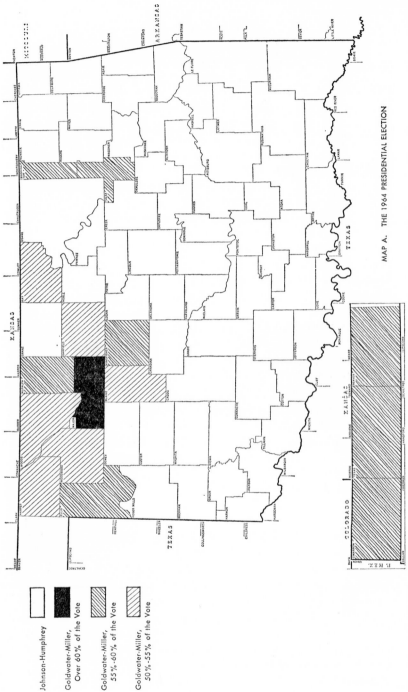

MAP A.   THE 1964 PRESIDENTIAL ELECTION

Johnson-Humphrey

Goldwater-Miller,
Over 60% of the Vote

Goldwater-Miller,
55%-60% of the Vote

Goldwater-Miller,
50%-55% of the Vote

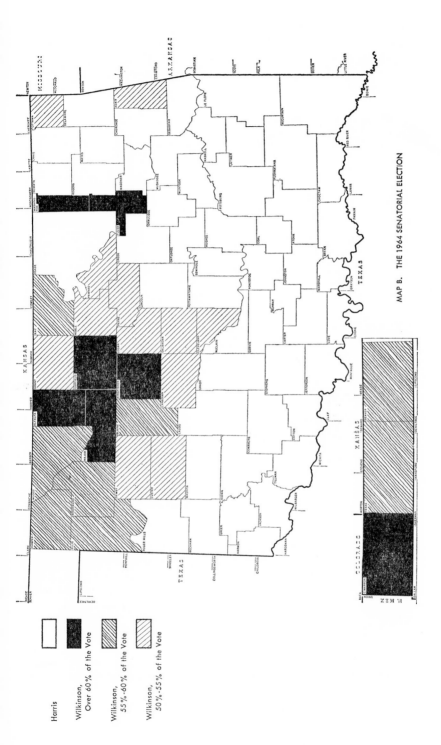

MAP B.   THE 1964 SENATORIAL ELECTION

Harris

Wilkinson,
Over 60% of the Vote

Wilkinson,
55%-60% of the Vote

Wilkinson,
50%-55% of the Vote

TABLE 7

DISTRIBUTION OF REPUBLICAN PARTY STRENGTH FOR PRESIDENT AND SENATE IN OKLAHOMA—1964

Fifteen Counties Wilkinson (Senate) Over 50% Goldwater (President) Over 50% of Vote						Twelve Counties Wilkinson (Senate) Over 50% Goldwater (President) Under 50% of Vote				
County	Wilkinson Percentage	Classification Senate Elections 1948-1962*	Goldwater Percentage	Classification Pres. Elections 1952-1960		County	Wilkinson Percentage	Classification Senate Elections 1948-1962*	Goldwater Percentage	Classification Pres. Elections 1952-1960
Alfalfa	64.5	SR	58.6	SR		Adair	53.5	LD	48.8	SR
Beaver	57.7	LR	56.8	SR		Canadian	52.8	LD	47.5	SR
Blaine	58.5	SR	53.5	SR		Cleveland	54.6	SD	45.4	SR
Cimmaron	60.5	LD	58.2	SR		Custer	50.9	SD	42.9	SR
Ellis	59.0	LR	56.4	SR		Dewey	53.7	LD	47.1	SR
Garfield	62.3	SR	54.7	SR		Grant	52.2	SR	48.4	SR
Harper	57.4	SR	52.6	SR		Logan	53.4	SR	46.9	SR
Kay	58.1	LR	51.6	SR		Noble	52.1	SR	44.3	SR
Kingfisher	62.5	SR	55.4	SR		Nowata	50.9	LD	44.8	SR
Major	60.8	SR	65.4	SR		Oklahoma	54.1	LD	48.0	SR
Texas	58.9	LD	57.2	SR		Pawnee	53.1	LR	48.8	SR
Tulsa	60.9	SR	55.5	SR		Payne	50.8	LD	47.1	SR
Washington	62.0	SR	59.1	SR						
Woods	58.6	LR	51.2	SR						
Woodward	58.3	SR	51.3	SR						

*Code: Strongly Republican (SR), 55% and Over
Leaning Republican (LR), 50-54.9%
Leaning Democratic (LD), 50-54.9%
Strongly Democratic (SD), 55% and Over

Source: *Oklahoma Votes, 1907-1962*, pp. 34-40, updated for the 1964 presidential and senatorial election.

The failure of Bud Wilkinson to disassociate himself from the national leaders of the Republican ticket seems to have been, in retrospect, a leading cause for his loss of the senate election to Fred R. Harris.

Wilkinson ran well in comparison with senatorial candidates on the Republican ballot since 1948. Based on senate elections from 1948-1962 he carired all twelve counties which are classified as strongly Republican, all five counties classified as leaning Republican, eight of twelve counties in the leaning Democratic classification, and won in two strongly Democratic counties—Custer and Cleveland.

Coattail Effect—Congressional Elections

Normal Democratic control of the state legislature has meant that each of the three congressional districtings has been accomplished in a manner which favors the dominant party.

The Democrats have secured 182 or 82% of the 222 congressional seats filled by regularly scheduled elections since statehood. Since 1948 the Democratic percentage of the total congressional vote has been 61% if districts where there was no contest due to absence of Republican opponents are eliminated. Again in 1964, Democratic candidates in contested districts (which excludes District 4) received 61% of the total vote, running considerably ahead of the presidential and senatorial candidates of their party. In non-presidential election years the Democratic percentage has run as high as 69.7% in 1958 and 65% in 1954. With John F. Kennedy heading the presidential ticket in 1960, the Democratic congressional percentage dropped to 55.8%.

Democrats were elected to office in five of the six congressional districts in the 1964 election. Republican Page Belcher was returned to office in the First District where Republican Party strength is concentrated, and received 63% of the vote. Democratic incumbents were reelected in the Second (Ed Edmondson), Third (Majority Leader Carl Albert), Fourth (Tom Steed-unopposed), and Fifth (John Jarman) Districts, and Jed Johnson, Jr. was elected in the Sixth District. The margins of victory ran from a low of Jed Johnson's 57% in the Sixth District to a high of 79% for Carl Albert in the Third District.

The youthful Jed Johnson, Jr. (he reached his 25th birthday only after the November election), son of a former Sixth District congressman, was opposed by the reactionary Bayard Auchincloss,

who had led a nationwide campaign for the "Sound Dollar" while
an economics teacher at an exclusive preparatory school in Oklahoma City's swank suburban Nichols Hills. Auchincloss con-
demned Johnson's student activity for the United Nations and
1959 Eisenhower Administration sponsored trip to Cuba after
Castro had taken power, as evidence of dangerous radicalism.[14]
Young Johnson received the active campaign support of Carl
Albert and Senator Mike Monroney. The radicalism issue seems
not to have strongly influenced the ranchers and farmers of Johnson's native western Oklahoma. Auchincloss had published a small
weekly newspaper and owned radio station KWCO in Chickasha.
He has since moved to Southern California where he seems to
think his political views are in harmony with the local population.

Coattail Effect–State Legislative Elections

   Normal party strength in the state legislature is one accepted
criterion of the party character of a given state. In August, 1964,
Governor Bellmon called state legislative special primary elections
for September 29 in order to comply with a federal district court
decision holding the May primaries, with few exceptions, to be
set aside and vacating the terms of holdover state senators. A
"sudden death" primary was held, without provision for a run-
off election, in order to have legislative candidates on the ballot
in November. The 30th session of the Oklahoma Legislature which
convened in January, 1965, is the first session apportioned as
nearly as possible on the basis of population in both houses since
statehood. Under the federal district court order fair representation on a population basis was granted to Tulsa and Oklahoma
counties in both House and Senate. Smaller counties which had
received one representative each in the House since 1931 were
combined in order to decrease their representation and provide
larger districts. With reapportionment it had been thought that
Republican strength, especially in Tulsa County, would be increased in the Legislature. Yet the party division in the 30th
Session failed to change significantly as comparison of the partisan composition of the legislature reveals (Table 8).

   The 1964 presidential election may not be an adequate measure
of an increase or decrease in Republican Party strength due to
the potential coattail effect. Perhaps it is surprising that the number of Republican legislators did not decrease substantially below
the previous session, in which the Republicans had increased their
strength due to the election of a Republican governor.

TABLE 8
PARTY COMPOSITION, OKLAHOMA STATE LEGISLATURE

			Senate
		No.	Percentage
29th Session	Democrat	38	77
(1963-1965)	Republican	6	13
		44	100
		No.	Percentage
30th Session	Democrat	41	85
(1965-1967)	Republican	7	15
		48	100
			House
		No.	Percentage
29th Session	Democrat	95	79
(1963-1965)	Republican	25	21
		120	100
		No.	Percentage
30th Session	Democrat	78	79
(1965-1967)	Republican	21	21
		99	100

THE 1964 CAMPAIGN IN OKLAHOMA

Democratic and Republican national party leaders campaigned extensively in Oklahoma during the 1964 presidential election. President Lyndon Johnson came to Oklahoma on Friday, September 25, and before a crowd estimated at 50,000 persons, dedicated the $120 million dollar Eufaula Dam and Reservoir. The Eufaula Dam is a key unit in the $1.2 billion dollar Arkansas River Navigation Project. President Johnson pledged that the project would continue on schedule. The afternoon of September 25, President Johnson and Lady Bird appeared in Oklahoma City before an audience estimated at 30,000. The occasion was the opening of the Oklahoma State Fair. These appearances were billed as "non-political," as the President campaigned behind the presidential seal. At a private President Club Reception for contributors of $1,000 or more to the Democratic Party a television film was made with Fred R. Harris, Senate candidate. The President requested, "Send me Fred Harris and we'll bring home the bacon and tack the coonskin to the wall."[15]

Hubert Humphrey, the Democratic Vice Presidential nominee came to Oklahoma and made speeches in Ardmore and Tulsa. In Tulsa, the metropolitan seat of Republicanism in the state, Humphrey hit hard at political extremism, charging that responsible Republican leaders had lost party control "to the apostles of discord and radicalism."[16]

Senator Barry Goldwater, the Republican presidential nominee, visited the state on September 22, and spoke to an audience estimated at 8,000 persons in Tulsa.[17] He criticized President Johnson for making his trip into the state at public expense under the guise of a "nonpolitical" tour. Goldwater attacked the foreign policy of the Johnson Administration, particularly the handling of the Viet Nam situation. He strongly endorsed the senate candidacy of Bud Wilkinson, and the candidacy of Republican Page Belcher, congressman in the First District. William Miller, the Vice Presidential candidate, spoke in Oklahoma City (September 28) and in Enid, Tulsa and Bartlesville (October 30).[18]

Richard Nixon, titular leader of the Republican Party, campaigned vigorously in Oklahoma as he did throughout the nation. He twice came to the state, and spoke in Enid, Tulsa and Oklahoma City.[19] The Nixon style of campaigning is felt by some to have been the most effective of any Republican national party leader during the Oklahoma campaign, especially as he encouraged Republicans to stay with the party. In his final appearance (November 2) Nixon attacked Hubert Humphrey—"Lyndon is no bargain—but when you add Hubert the price is too high." Bud Wilkinson was praised as a "leader of men" while Nixon referred to Fred Harris as a "run-of-the-mill politician."[20]

President Eisenhower was scheduled to appear in Oklahoma City on October 26 in a speech postponed first due to the death of former President Herbert Hoover and then cancelled when Eisenhower became ill. The text of the speech was released and it strongly endorsed the senate candidacy of Bud Wilkinson. Referring to his own early attempts at coaching (St. Mary's in Texas, and Ft. Meade, Maryland) Eisenhower said, "If an average sort of football coach can get to the White House, why should not an outstanding football coach go to the United States Senate."[21] Wilkinson seems to have answered this question aptly in a press conference after election day when he explained his loss with the summary, "I didn't get enough votes."[22]

The key to interest on the part of national party leaders in coming to Oklahoma may have been less the concern over the presidential vote than the closely contested race for the Senate seat. The Democrats wanted to make sure that what had long been safe Democratic territory did not send a Republican senator to Washington, D. C. Bud Wilkinson had been urged by Barry Goldwater and Dwight D. Eisenhower to enter politics and seek the senate nomination for the Republican Party. The early prediction that they had a winner was not without considerable basis, as indicated by the close outcome of the election. Wilkinson, disappointed after his loss and looking for a job, stated it thus: "I was sincerely convinced I would win." He had, therefore, made no other post-election plans.[23]

Oklahoma Republicans had entered the 1964 presidential and senatorial campaign with a note of high enthusiasm. By mid-February the Oklahoma delegates to the Republican National Convention were pledged in district and state convention to Senator Barry Goldwater.[24] They were the first state delegation in the nation formally committed and it was over the opposition of Governor Henry Bellmon, Oklahoma's first Republican governor. Bellmon had sponsored a move at the State Convention to leave the delegation unpledged and consequently invoked the ire of what was a nearly unanimous group of enthusiastic Goldwater supporters. Governor Bellmon served as chairman of the Republican delegation and the delegates were rewarded for their early endorsement with favorable seats near the front of San Francisco's Cow Palace as the convention nominated Barry Goldwater on the first ballot.

The delegation to the Democratic National Convention in Atlantic City was united under the leadership of state chairman Smith Hester. They added their voice to the unanimous selection of Lyndon B. Johnson as the party standard bearer.[25] The Democrats were wiser after loss of the governorship to Republican Henry Bellmon in 1962. They entered the general election in a spirit of party harmony. Former Governor Gary had supported Harris in the run-off primary, and Senator J. Howard Edmondson, in defeat, also pledged his support to the election of Harris.[26]

Fred R. Harris, born on a southern Oklahoma farm, worked his way through the University of Oklahoma. He earned degrees in history, government and law, receiving the honors of Phi Beta Kappa and Order of the Coif. He had served in the state senate for eight years, and in 1962 had unsuccessfully sought the Democratic nomination for governor in the primary, coming in a strong fifth in the election.[27]

Opposing Harris in the November election was Bud Wilkinson, one of the most famous football coaches in the nation. Wilkinson was a native Minnesotan and received his B.A. from the University of Minnesota and M.A. in English from Syracuse University. Oklahoma Republicans had been jubilant in January when Charles B. Wilkinson, long rumored as a possible senatorial candidate, legally changed his name to Bud Wilkinson, his party registration from Democrat to Republican, and resigned as Athletic Director and head football coach at the University of Oklahoma. He had been the head football coach for 17 years. His primary governmental experience had been service as head of the President's Council on Physical Fitness for three years.[28]

Football and politics became intertwined as the capability of Coach Wilkinson to become Senator was debated, rehashed and rerun like a football playback on Sunday T.V. Some student supporters of Fred R. Harris distributed "Beat Barry, Bud, and Texas" bumper stickers. Others paraded "bumper" politics with "I'm for Fred Harris and Gomer." These were later withdrawn by Harris headquarters after the protests of Gomer Jones, Wilkinson's successor, that he in fact supported Bud's candidacy for the Senate.

When asked by Gaylord Shaw, Associated Press writer, about the major issues in the campaign, Harris answered by saying, "pay checks and peace," while Wilkinson's reply was "growth and centralization of power in Washington."[29] While Harris stressed "jobs" and "national security" as the most basic issues facing Oklahoma, his opponent Wilkinson campaigned against the extreme liberalism of Hubert Humphrey, linked him to the ADA, and asked, ". . . do we want to preserve the republic with the benefits of limited government and with limited regulation of the farm, the pasture, the oil rigs and the individual citizen's freedom of action?" Wilkinson felt that we must, and stressed a philosophy of government based on the 10th Amendment to the Constitution and the importance of individual responsibility.

Stands taken by the senatorial candidates on several issues in the campaign were similar. Both favored the Kerr-Mills program of medical care for the aged, although Harris favored minor amendments. Harris was supported by members of former Robert S. Kerr's family in seeking the office which appeared to make his endorsement of this major legislative accomplishment necessary.

Such matters as the retention of the 27½% depletion allowable and development of the Arkansas River Navigation Project found the candidates in basic harmony.[30]

The issues which separated Harris and Wilkinson included civil rights legislation, federal aid to education, further tax cuts, foreign aid programs and delegation of presidential control over nuclear weapons. The Republican and Democratic national party platforms were normally taken as the cue for the Oklahoma campaigners on these issues.[31]

Harris tied his campaign closely to that of Johnson for the presidency, apparent both in his advertising (Harris-LBJ) and stands taken on most issues. Occasionally, issue positions were moderated to a slightly more conservative view in accord with the candidate's interpretation of his constituents' views. Bud Wilkinson, not so experienced a campaigner as Harris, followed the Goldwater-Miller brand of Republicanism. When asked if he was in "full accord" with the national ticket his reply was "I concur with the general philosophy of the ticket and Republican platform."[32] Wilkinson in some instances appeared to espouse Goldwater Republicanism more effectively than the presidential candidate himself. Use of analogies to the "fall of Rome" were not unusual in his speeches. In Yukon, early in October, Wilkinson stated, "The major reasons for the Roman fall—undermining the home, high taxes, decay of religion and decay within the state—are issues just as important to Americans today as they were to Romans."[33] Eventually, the "fall of Rome" issue was counter-attacked by Harris.

After Harris accepted a Wilkinson challenge to debate, the two candidates appeared October 15 on Tulsa station KTUL-TV.[34] The debate was carried throughout the state and lasted for thirty minutes. Although the outcome must remain indecisive as to whether or not doubtful voters were swayed to one or the other candidate, the two contenders hit hard at their earlier charges against one another. Harris stressed his opponent's lack of political experience. Wilkinson attacked Harris' attendance record in the 1963 state legislative session. Harris charged that Wilkinson "talks about big government and federal handouts," adding: "I say let him tell us which handouts he would eliminate." Wilkinson saw the major issue as "who is going to be the best representative for Oklahoma. That's what we are going to talk about. . . . Who do you want to put in the game?"[35]

A side effect of the senate campaign may have been increased faculty participation in politics at the University of Oklahoma. Regents' rules demand that a faculty member resign to seek partisan political office. Bud Wilkinson resigned in order to comply with the rules governing partisan political involvement. Inevitably, a period of lengthy service at the University of Oklahoma became a debated subject of his qualifications and suitability of public office. A committee of nine professors endorsed Wilkinson for the Senate, and subsequently massive faculty and student support was claimed for the former coach.[36] This was offset by an advertisement in the *Daily Oklahoman* and *Oklahoma Times*, signed by 209 faculty and staff members, headed "OU Faculty & Staff strongly support Fred R. Harris for U.S. Senate."[37] This advertisement was attacked on the editorial pages of *The Norman Transcript*.[38] Signers of the advertisement were charged with attempting to discredit Bud Wilkinson in his own community. Fear of loss of funds and support for a $20 million dollar endowment fund, the "Plan for Excellence," was mentioned.[39] University President George L. Cross commented publically on the wording of the advertisement.[40] Governor Henry Bellmon defended the right of state employees, at least those not hired under the merit system, to exercise their rights in political controversies.[41]

POLLS

Otis Sullivant, the veteran political columnist on the *Daily Oklahoman* staff was remarkably accurate in polls taken during the 1952, 1956 and 1960 presidential elections.[42] His polls do not attempt to cover the entire state, and the representative basis of his samplings has been questioned. The polls are sometimes taken on mainstreet and in shopping districts and may overrepresent a conservative point of view. The Sullivant poll published October 25, 1964, was conducted in 17 counties over a two week period.[43] Washington and Tulsa counties, both strongly Republican, were not included in the poll. With 3,329 samples, Sullivant predicted 62.1% of the vote for Johnson, and 37.9% for Goldwater. This overestimated the Johnson vote in Oklahoma by 6.4%.

Sullivant was more accurate in predicting the outcome of the Senate race between Harris and Wilkinson.[44] In the 17-county poll of October 25, 1964, he indicated that Harris would poll 52.9% of the vote on the basis of 3,316 samples. Harris actually received 51.5% of the vote and the poll was 1.8% off, overestimating Harris' strength but within a reasonable margin of error.

The samples taken on two different occasions in Oklahoma county are significant due to the large vote in that county and its history as a "swing" county in statewide elections.[45] Again, Sullivant overestimated the Johnson vote in Oklahoma county as he did in the aforementioned polls (Table 9). The polls in Oklahoma county for the U.S. Senate race predicted that Bud Wilkinson would win in the county but underestimated his percentage margin of victory. The second poll, October 24, showed a 1.4% gain on Wilkinson's behalf over the poll of September 9-10. Wilkinson won the county by 55.4% of the vote, and the final Sullivant poll was within a reasonable margin of error (Table 9).

TABLE 9
OKLAHOMA COUNTY SAMPLES
PRESIDENTIAL ELECTION OF 1964

Sept. 9-10	No.	%	Oct. 24	No.	%	% Actual Vote	
Johnson	473	61.6	Johnson	460	56	Johnson	52
Goldwater	296	38.5	Goldwater	361	44	Goldwater	48

OKLAHOMA COUNTY SAMPLES
SENATE ELECTION OF 1964

Sept. 9-10	No.	%	Oct. 24	No.	%	% Actual Vote	
Wilkinson	385	51.5	Wilkinson	429	52.9	Wilkinson	55.4
Harris	326	48.5	Harris	382	41.7	Harris	44.6

A group of political science students at the University of Oklahoma conducted a poll at the request of Sorin-Hall, Inc., a Washington, D.C. public relations firm. On the basis of three different samplings of approximately 400 voters each, spaced two weeks apart, they came up with an accurate sampling. The loosely constructed survey included stratification on the basis of income, sex, race, and rural or urban residence. The sample did not cover the entire state, but did include voters in the six congressional districts and in widely separated cities such as Muskogee, Atoka, Altus, Lawton, Chickasha, Enid, Tulsa, and a heavy concentration in Oklahoma and Cleveland counties. The survey was a little more than 2% low in indicating the margin of Johnson's victory in the state, but was almost exact in predicting 51.5% of the vote for Harris in the Senate race, only .4% high (Table 10).

TABLE 10

POLL—SORIN-HALL, INC.

Number	Presidential	Official Vote	Survey
1200 (Approx.)	Johnson	55.75%	53.3%
	Goldwater	44.25%	33.3%
	Undecided		13.4%

Number	Senatorial	Official Vote	Survey
1200 (Approx.)	Harris	51.1%	51.5%
	Wilkinson	48.9%	44.3%
	Undecided		4.2%

The survey conducted by University of Oklahoma students revealed a high percentage of undecided voters in the presidential election. Many of these persons never reach a decision and will be found in the non-voting category. The students had considerable difficulty interviewing some reluctant persons in the middle and upper income areas and met eagerness on the part of lower-middle income, and Negro voters especially, to be interviewed. The best indications for the final shift of the undecided voters toward Republican Barry Goldwater, but an unwillingness to reveal their preferences, may be found in the voter's attachment to the Democratic party identification. In certain areas, such as Atoka, McAlester, and Muskogee, normally strongly Democratic, indecisiveness seems to have been closely related to concern over Johnson's stand on civil rights, implying a minor incidence of "white backlash." It is a matter of speculation that some of the undecided voters had reached a decision but were unwilling to reveal their preference to anyone and concealed it for the secrecy of the voting booth.

NEGRO VOTE

Negroes voted with a large degree of unanimity for the Johnson-Humphrey ticket in Oklahoma, according to available information. Otis Sullivant polled the Negro area of Muskogee in eastern Oklahoma in his October 22 survey and found 27 of 30 Negroes favored the Democratic candidate for President over Goldwater. In the Senate race 23 favored Harris over Wilkinson.[46] Students who worked in the Sorin-Hall, Inc. poll discovered a high interest among Negro interviewees, and a similar division as to political preferences in the election.

The 1960 census indicates that 6.6% of Oklahoma's total population is Negro.[47] Negro residents are concentrated in McCurtain, McIntosh, Choctaw and Muskogee counties, in addition to the metropolitan areas, Tulsa and Oklahoma City. The 1961 Report of the Civil Rights Commission includes Oklahoma among those southern and border states where no discrimination has been found with reference to registration and voting on the basis of race.[48] Negro organization leaders worked along with party workers, especially Democratic workers, in Oklahoma City in an attempt to get a large number of their voters to the polls. Ward 2 in Oklahoma City (about two-thirds of the 68 precincts are populated with Negro voters) returned 19,328 votes for Johnson and 10,430 votes for Goldwater. The typical vote in a Negro precinct would be Johnson, 400 (97%), and Goldwater, 10 votes (3%). Ward 2 returned 16,410 votes for Harris as compared to 11,264 for Wilkinson in the Senate race—ticket splitting was in evidence. Johnson polled 64.9% of the vote in Ward 2; Harris 59.3% to fall behind by 5.6%. It is worth noting that 2,084 voters cast ballots for Johnson in Ward 2 without voting for a candidate in the senate election.[49]

VOTER TURNOUT

There has been some tendency for voter turnout to increase and in 1952 the all time high was reached in the election which placed Dwight D. Eisenhower in the White House and Oklahoma in the Republican column for the first time since 1928. The previous high

TABLE 12

AVERAGE PERCENTAGE OF VOTER TURNOUT FOR THE STATE IN PRESIDENTIAL ELECTIONS SINCE 1948 BASED ON VOTING AGE POPULATION[50]

Presidential Election	Turnout	Percentage, Voting Age Population
1948	721,599	52.3
1952	948,984	68.3
1956	859,350	61.2
1960	903,150	63.7
1964	932,499	64.1

Source: *Oklahoma Votes, 1907-1962*, pp. 67-68, updated for 1964 presidential election.

in Oklahoma had been in 1940 when the turnout reached 60.3% but turnout had dropped in the elections of 1944 and 1948. The 1964 presidential election marked the second highest number of voters to go to the polls in the state's history, and the percentage of voting age population was 64.1%. If estimates of increase in voting age population are relatively accurate for 1964 then little significant increase in voter turnout has taken place since 1960.

If voter turnout is calculated on the basis of registered voters it would be 72.3% for the 1964 presidential election. This is thought to be too high an estimate. Voter registrations are a relatively accurate basis for comparisons of party strength. However, voter registration is suspect on a basis for figuring voter turnout in Oklahoma. Central registration data were not maintained by the State Election Board until 1960. County election boards are frequently unable to keep their rolls current. Indeed, in 19 counties (1964) registered voters exceed the census reports of population 21 years of age and over.

Conclusions

This analysis demonstrates that party identification was the primary stabilizing factor in the 1964 presidential election. The "reinstatement" effect is used to indicate a return to the Democratic Party in the presidential election. Oklahoma voters had cast a majority of their votes for Republican presidential candidates in 1952, 1956 and 1960. The "maintaining" concept is used to indicate the maintenance of Democratic Party strength in senatorial, congressional and state legislative elections. Certainly, little significant change in party strength is evident in the congressional and state legislative elections of 1964.

The 1964 Johnson victory in Oklahoma indicates the influence on voting of party identification based on past voting behavior as distinguished from party identification based on registration. Johnson's Oklahoma vote lagged 5.7% behind his national average of 61.4% of the two-party vote. The vote for Johnson approximates the normal expectation of the Democratic vote for a presidential contender in the state if the period of 1932-1964 is taken as a guide. During this period 55.8% of the presidential vote has been Democratic as compared with 55.75% for Johnson in 1964.

May 55.8% of the total vote be considered the normal expectation of Democratic vote in presidential elections? Is it a measure of Democratic party identification reflected in voting? A problem is encountered in using 1932-1964 as a base period or means of establishing an "equilibrium" situation. The percentage of Democratic presidential vote has varied from 73.2% for Franklin D. Roosevelt in 1932 to 40.9% for John F. Kennedy in 1960. Only the elections of 1940, 1944 and 1964 approximate an average of 55%-57%. Probably, Oklahoma voters will continue to respond to broader national trends when voting in presidential elections. Each presidential election in Oklahoma will continue to have its own special characteristics and present the unusual situation, relatively, rather than an "equilibrium" situation as in the 1964 election.

In the 1964 presidential election in Oklahoma a salient feature was the normal party identification of the voter, as reflected in past voting behavior. The vote for Goldwater-Miller diminished (when compared with the elections of 1952, 1956 and 1960) in areas of the state which traditionally have been strongly Republican. Comparatively, in 1960 when John F. Kennedy lost the state for the Democrats, an almost similar situation occurred. Kennedy received 40.9% of the vote and a majority of the vote in only 14 counties. With minor exceptions, these were counties in "Little Dixie" and on the Texas border. This was the strong Democratic vote within the state which even the religious issue could not dislodge. Between these two extremes, which have operated within a period of four years in Oklahoma, rests the mean—the voters are normally Democratic, but will, due to national trends, attractive personalities, economic issues, the religious issue and return to peace, switch to the opposite party in presidential elections with scarcely a second thought.

What long range trends are apparent in Oklahoma after the votes in the 1964 presidential and senatorial elections have been counted? Although identification with party played an important role in the 1964 elections, the results of recent presidential elections (1952, 1956, 1960), the gubernatorial election (1962) and in some respects the senatorial election (1964) indicate that party identification is not as important a factor in every election. Recent elections offer some justification to think that Oklahoma voters have become less conscious of traditional identification with the Democratic party as based on registration and past voting behavior. There is a suggestion that the nature of the party system is undergoing change and that the Republicans have increased their competitive position since 1952, in order better to contest the vote in presidential, gubernatorial and senatorial elections. This increase in competitive position is not yet apparent at the level of lesser state offices and in state legislative elections.

The senatorial election of 1964 in Oklahoma is significant from the standpoint of indicating an increase in Republican party strength. Wilkinson might have won the senate election except for the presidential "coattails" which reacted to benefit his Democratic opponent, Fred R. Harris. Wilkinson's own predisposition to follow unwittingly the releases of national Republican party headquarters enabled his opposition to label him a "right wing back." The Republican senatorial candidate's inability or unwillingness to break with Goldwater-Miller Republicanism, referred to as "conservatism," led to his downfall in Oklahoma. Nativism in Oklahoma politics is accented rather than deemphasized. After 17 years in the state, both Wilkinson and Auchincloss (Sixth District) were still considered by some voters to be "carpetbaggers." Wilkinson by any standard—Democratic or Republican—was a political novice, if an effective one. Wilkinson's shock at losing the senate election could be compared to that of OU football fans in 1958 when Notre Dame snapped the team's 47 game winning streak.

The Democratic party within Oklahoma is factional in character. When Republican party successes in presidential elections penetrate the state, Democratic party disunity is increased and becomes divisive. Party leaders were united, relatively, in the election of 1964 and this was of primary importance for a victory in the senate race. The Republicans as the minority party in the state suffer from factionalism and disunity, injurious in the development of a strong opposition party. To use the Lubell analogy, the Republicans can rarely break apart the "Democratic sun" in order to form a temporary coalition and elect the governor or U.S. senator.

FOOTNOTES

[2] Austin Ranney and Willmore Kendall, "The American Party Systems," *The American Political Science Review*, Vol. XLVIII (June, 1954), p. 483.

[3] Philip E. Converse, Angus Campbell, Warren E. Miller, Donald E. Stokes, "Stability and Change in 1960: A Reinstating Election," *The American Political Science Review*, Vol. LV (June, 1961), p. 280.

[4] *The Norman Transcript*, Wednesday, January 29, 1964, p. 1.

[5] Samuel Lubell, *The Future of American Politics* (2d ed. rev.; Garden City, N.Y.: Doubleday Anchor Books, 1956), pp. 210-218.

[6] *Oklahoma Votes, 1907-1962*, op. cit., p. 53.

[7] Harry Holloway, "Oklahoma Goes Republican," *Bureau of Government Research Bulletin*, Vol. 1, No. 2 (June, 1963), pp. 1-3.

[8] V. O. Key, Jr., *American State Politics: An Introduction* (New York: Alfred A. Knopf, 1956), p. 221.

[9] Paul T. David, et. al., ed., *Presidential Nominating Politics in 1952, The South* (Baltimore: the Johns Hopkins Press, 1954), p. 295. (Cortez A. M. Ewing and June Benson, "Oklahoma").

[10] U. S. Bureau of the Census, *Oklahoma General Population Characteristics,* 1960, pp. 28, 29.

[11] Wayne Young, "Oklahoma Politics: With Special Reference to the Election of Oklahoma's first Republican Governor." Unpublished doctoral dissertation, Department of Government, University of Oklahoma, 1964, pp. 48-49.

[12] *Ibid.,* p. 49.

[13] Angus Campbell, Philip E. Converse, Warren E. Miller, Donald E. Stokes, *The American Voter* (New York: John Wiley & Sons, Inc., 1960), p. 531.

[14] *The Daily Oklahoman,* October 31, 1964, p. 13.

[15] *The Daily Oklahoman,* Sept. 26, 1964, p. 1.

[16] *The Daily Oklahoman,* Oct. 20, 1964, p. 1.

[17] *The Daily Oklahoman,* Sept. 23, 1964, p. 1.

[18] *The Daily Oklahoman,* Sept. 29, 1964, p. 1; Oct. 31, 1964, p. 1.

[19] *The Daily Oklahoman,* Oct. 22, 1964, p. 1; Nov. 3, 1964, p. 1.

[20] *Ibid.*

[21] *The Norman Transcript,* Oct. 23, 1964, p. 1.

[22] *The Daily Oklahoman,* Nov. 5, 1964, p. 9.

[23] *Ibid.*

[24] *The Sunday Oklahoman,* Feb. 16, 1964, p. 1.

[25] *The Daily Oklahoman,* Aug. 27, 1964, p. 1.

[26] *The Daily Oklahoman,* June 28, 1964, p. 17.

[27] *The Norman Transcript,* Oct. 22, 1964, p. 5.

[28] *Ibid.*

[29] *The Sunday Oklahoman,* Oct. 4, 1964, p. 4A.

[30] *Ibid.*

[31] *Ibid.*

[32] *The Daily Oklahoman,* Sept. 17, 1964, p. 6.

[33] *The Daily Oklahoman,* Oct. 9, 1964, p. 3.

[34] *The Norman Transcript,* Oct. 16, 1964, p. 2.

[35] *Ibid.*

[36] *Oklahoma Journal,* Oct. 20, 1964, p. 1.

[37] *The Daily Oklahoman,* Oct. 17, 1964; *Oklahoma City Times,* Oct. 16, 1964, p. 8.

[38] *The Norman Transcript,* Oct. 20, 1964, p. 4.

[39] *Ibid.*

[40] *The Sunday Oklahoman,* Oct. 18, 1964, p. 1.

[41] *The Daily Oklahoman,* Oct. 20, 1964, p. 5.

[42] *The Sunday Oklahoman,* Oct. 25, 1964, pp. 1, 2.

[43] *Ibid.*

[44] *Ibid.*

[45] *The Daily Oklahoman,* Oct. 24, 1964, p. 1.

[46] *The Daily Oklahoman,* Oct. 20, 1964, p. 40.

[47] Census Bureau, Oklahoma: *General Population Characteristics,* 1960, p. 31.

[48] *1961 U. S. Commission on Civil Rights Report,* p. 102.

[49] Statistics for Ward 2 are from Secretary, State Election Board.

[50] Eligible voting population is defined as persons 21 and over. These turnout figures are based on U. S. census data, with interpolations by fifths for even-numbered years between the regular decennial censuses, and an extrapolation by two-fifths of the 1950-1960 decennial change in population for 1964. This method was used in order to provide turnout estimates for 1964 which would be comparable to those in *Oklahoma Votes, 1907-1962.*

The 1964 Presidential Election in Kansas: A Report

MARVIN HARDER

Wichita State University

A Deviating Election.—Kansans have participated in twenty-six presidential elections. In nineteen of them (73 per cent), Republican presidential candidates carried the state. Not since 1936 has a non-Republican candidate won the state's electoral votes. Therefore it is appropriate to describe the 1964 presidential election in Kansas, in which President Johnson received 53.1 per cent of the two-party vote, as a *deviating* election.

General Weaver, the Populist, carried Kansas in 1892. William Jennings Bryan was also successful in 1896. Woodrow Wilson received a plurality of the votes in both 1912 and 1916, and so won the electoral votes of Kansas twice. Franklin Roosevelt bettered Wilson's feat by winning majorities in both 1932 and 1936.

Senator Goldwater and his running mate, Congressman Miller, received 46.9 per cent of the total two-party vote cast in Kansas in the 1964 election. This figure represents a 13.8 per cent decline from Richard Nixon's percentage in 1960, and an even greater reduction from the percentages received by General Eisenhower in 1952 and 1956.

TABLE 1

PER CENT OF TWO-PARTY VOTE RECEIVED BY REPUBLICAN PRESIDENTIAL CANDIDATES IN THE LAST FIVE ELECTIONS

1948	1952	1956	1960	1964
54.6	69.3	65.7	60.7	46.9

The deviating character of the 1964 election in Kansas is further revealed by a comparison of the number of counties carried by Democratic presidential candidates in each of the last five elections. President Johnson won nearly as many counties as President Roosevelt won in 1936, and he came within .8 per cent of equalling Roosevelt's winning margin of 53.9 per cent.

It is virtually impossible to determine the precise number of Republican identifiers who voted for President Johnson, but it is

TABLE 2

NUMBER OF COUNTIES WON BY DEMOCRATIC PRESIDENTIAL
CANDIDATES IN THE LAST FIVE ELECTIONS

1948	1952	1956	1960	1964
7	1	1	2	62

probable that more than ten per cent of them did so. This estimate
is based upon a comparison of Senator Goldwater's percentage
with that usually garnered by Republican candidates for minor
state offices. For example, the median percentage of the two-party
vote received by Republican candidates for Secretary of State
since 1896 is 58 per cent. Assuming that this figure reflects the
usual ratio of Republican to Democratic identifiers in the state,
it is not unlikely that more than one out of every ten Kansas
Republicans voted for President Johnson and Senator Humphrey.

A *Reinstating Election.*—At the same time, the gubernatorial
and all five congressional contests were won by Republican candidates. This fact suggests that no significant realignment occurred,
that the balance of power in Kansas party politics remains substantially what it has been for more than a century.

That is not to say, however, that Senator Goldwater's candidacy left the numbers of Republican and Democratic identifiers
unchanged. An as yet undetermined number of Republicans
actually changed their party affiliation. Moreover, it is possible
that more Negro voters than ever before now regard themselves
as Democrats. But such shifts could not have been significantly
numerous, otherwise Republican candidates for congressional and
state offices would have fared less well than they did.

Split-ticket voting is a common phenomenon in Kansas elections,
perhaps in part because it is not possible to pull one lever or mark
one x and vote for all of the candidates of one party. The dimensions of split-ticket voting are revealed by the fact that in 1960
President Kennedy lost Sedgwick County (Wichita) by some
14,000 votes while at the same time the Democratic congressional
candidate lost it by only 3,000 votes and the Democratic candidate for Lieutenant-Governor carried the county by 14,000 votes.
In the 1964 election William Avery, the victorious Republican
gubernatorial candidate, ran eight percentage points ahead of the
Goldwater-Miller team in more than one-half of the state's 105
counties. In one county (Lane) Avery's percentage of the guber-

natorial vote was twenty-two percentage points higher than Senator Goldwater's percentage.

Aside from President Johnson's victory, the 1964 general election in Kansas was a *reinstating* election. Not only did the Republicans win all five congressional seats and all state administrative offices; they also retained firm control of both Houses of the Kansas Legislature. The Democrats gained five seats in the Senate and six seats in the House.

TABLE 3

PARTY COMPOSITION OF THE STATE LEGISLATURE

Senate (40)		House (125)	
Republicans	27	Republicans	80
Democrats	13	Democrats	45

It was a reinstating election in still another respect. The counties in which President Johnson received sixty or more per cent of the vote were all counties which in the past have fallen in the upper Democratic quartile (based on per cent of total vote received by Democratic candidates for major offices). Ellis and Wyandotte counties, traditionally the strongest Democratic counties in the state, again gave the Democratic candidates their largest winning margins.

TABLE 4

COUNTIES IN WHICH JOHNSON-HUMPHREY TICKET
RECEIVED MORE THAN 60 PER CENT OF VOTE

County	Percent
Ellis	71
Wyandotte	68
Pawnee	64
Reno	63
Rush	62
Crawford	62
Miami	61
Morton	61
Rice	61
Cherokee	60
Barton	60
Edwards	60
Ellsworth	60
Gray	60
Ness	60

TABLE 5

COUNTIES IN WHICH THE GOLDWATER-MILLER TICKET
RECEIVED 55 OR MORE PER CENT OF THE VOTE

County	Percent
Clay	62
Norton	61
Waubaunsee	59
Hamilton	58
Brown	57
Rawlins	57
Greenwood	57
Washington	57
Chautauqua	56
Cheyenne	56
Coffey	56
Elk	56
Johnson	55
Phillips	55

A look at the counties in which Senator Goldwater polled 55 or more per cent of the vote again confirms the expected. The Goldwater-Miller ticket ran best in seven counties on or near the Nebraska border and in three cattle-raising counties of the Flint Hills region. These are counties, as the saying goes, in which it is hard to find a Democrat.

Who Defected?—The study of election returns can yield clues which are helpful in discovering the short term influences which are operative in an election. A preliminary analysis of county and precinct election returns in Kansas produced two general findings: (1) nearly all of the Negro voters in Kansas supported the Johnson-Humphrey ticket; (2) some Republican identifiers in all social and economic groups defected from the Republican ticket, including wealthier than average suburbanites.

In 1952 the only precincts in the city of Wichita which were won by Adlai Stevenson were Negro precincts. He carried these precincts by margins ranging from 71 to 83 per cent. In 1964 President Johnson secured virtually all of the Negro vote.[1] For example, in two precincts the final tally produced the following results:

TABLE 6

NEGRO VOTE IN TWO WICHITA PRECINCTS

Precinct and Ward No.	Johnson-Humphrey	Goldwater-Miller
17th of 4	366	4
19th of 4	520	1

Because there was a sharp reduction in the Republican percentages of the presidential vote in most Kansas counties, it is a reasonable hypothesis that Republican defectors came from every socio-economic group. This includes the wealthier-than-average suburbanites. In Johnson County (often called the "bedroom of Kansas City") for example, the Goldwater-Miller ticket received only 55 per cent of the vote. In previous presidential elections Johnson County gave Republican candidates more than 70 per cent of the vote.

As anticipated, the two principal metropolitan counties in Kansas, Sedgwick (Wichita) and Wyandotte (Kansas City), gave President Johnson substantial majorities of their presidential vote. The President won Sedgwick County by a margin of more than 13,000 votes and Wyandotte by more than 20,000. He might have carried Sedgwick by an even greater margin if heavy rains beginning in the early afternoon hours of election day had not reduced the turn-out. It is estimated that the rains reduced the Sedgwick County total vote by some 17,000. Democratic leaders in Wichita believe that the rain saved several incumbent Republican judges from defeat, arguing that a substantial portion of the working class population usually votes between the hours of five and seven in the afternoon.

Catholic precincts went Democratic by larger margins than in any previous election. This fact suggests that some Republican identifiers of Catholic persuasion defected to the Johnson-Humphrey ticket. For example, in rural, Catholic Sherman Township in Sedgwick County, the Democratic ticket received 79 per cent of the vote. This statistic is particularly interesting in view of the fact that Sherman Township is a fairly prosperous farming community.

Equally interesting is the fact that two of the most Republican counties in the central part of Kansas, Harvey and McPherson, were carried by President Johnson, while Senator Goldwater easily carried adjoining Marion County. Since a sizeable proportion of the population of all three counties are Mennonites, and Mennonites traditionally vote Republican, these differences beg explanation. It is possible that the unprecedented endorsement given the Johnson-Humphrey ticket by leaders of the Western Division of the General Conference of Mennonite Churches accounts for the deviation of Harvey and McPherson counties. Many of the Mennonites in Marion County belong to a different conference and one in which the leaders did not endorse the Democratic ticket.

Coattail Effect.—While it is true that every Democratic congressional candidate in Kansas in 1964 identified himself in speeches and advertisements as a Johnson supporter, and while it is also true that three of the four incumbent Republican congressmen won by margins less than what they received two years earlier, it is not necessarily true that the Democratic candidates polled larger percentages than their predecessors because of their identification with the President. There are other variables to be considered. A reverse coattail influence may have been operative: three of the four incumbents had endorsed Senator Goldwater prior to his nomination at San Francisco. Their Democratic opponents advertised this fact at every opportunity. And there is an additional possibility that Republican defectors to Johnson supported Republican congressional candidates in greater numbers than they might otherwise have done, either because they feared a reduced Republican membership in Congress or because by this means they could salve their consciences.

Voter Turnout.—Some experienced political observers in Kansas had predicted that a significant number of voters would stay home from the polls because they were dissatisfied with both presidential candidates. By the middle of the morning on election day it was apparent that this prediction would not come true. Lines had formed at most polling places from the moment the doors were opened. A heavy vote seemed in the offing. But by mid-afternoon heavy rains blanketed parts of south-central and eastern Kansas. The result was a total turnout in Kansas of about 830,000 voters, some 100,000 less than the figure predicted by the Secretary of State.

Extremist Activity.—The rules of fair play were frequently violated during the campaign period preceding the election. Large quantities of "hate literature" were distributed by one means or another. Many of these pieces contained ill-concealed appeals to anti-semitic and anti-Negro prejudices. Some attempted to associate the Democrats with the Communist Party. Most of such handouts were signed by organizations like The Christian Crusade and by various Citizens for Goldwater groups. There is no readily-obtainable evidence that such appeals had any appreciable effect.

Newspaper Endorsements.—There are four major daily newspapers in Kansas: the *Kansas City Star,* the *Hutchinson News-Herald,* the *Wichita Eagle* and *Beacon,* and the *Topeka Daily Capital* and *Journal.* The first two editorialized in favor of President Johnson and Senator Humphrey; the last two editorially endorsed Senator Goldwater and Congressman Miller. Two of the papers encouraged split-ticket voting, however. The *Hutchinson News-Herald* endorsed the Republican gubernatorial candidate and the *Wichita Eagle* endorsed the Democratic gubernatorial candidate.

Some of the other daily newspapers with less circulation than the big four also took stands on the presidential contest. For example, the *Parsons Sun,* published by Clyde Reed, Jr., a former Republican gubernatorial candidate, withheld its support from the Goldwater-Miller ticket. So too did the *Salina Journal,* edited by another prominent Republican, Whitley Austin.

Short of a survey of voter motivations, it would be impossible to make any estimate as to the influence of these newspaper editorials. It is interesting to note, however, that Reno County (Hutchinson) gave the President 63 per cent of its vote; at the same time, it gave the Democratic gubernatorial candidate, Harry Wiles, only 52 per cent of its vote. The endorsement of the Republican gubernatorial candidate by the *News* may have had an impact, since Reno County is, in a sense, the home territory of Harry Wiles. The friends and neighbors variable should have helped Wiles garner a larger vote in Reno County than he did.

The *Eagle's* endorsement of Harry Wiles surprised many Wichitans. Since William Avery had publicly supported Senator Goldwater, and the *Eagle* endorsed Goldwater, it would have been consistent for the *Eagle* to have supported Avery. The fact that it did not reflects a particular interest of many Wichitans who have long believed that the Topeka-Kansas City axis has dominated Kansas government, often at the expense of the citizens of south-central Kansas. This attitude was reflected in the Republican gubernatorial primary in August when Sedgwick County voters gave one of Avery's primary opponents, Senator Paul Wunsch, a three to one majority. Senator Wunsch, a resident of adjoining Kingman County, had identified himself with the interests of Wichita by supporting the inclusion of the University of Wichita into the State's system of higher education.

Conclusion.—The results of the 1964 general election in Kansas were consistent with the historic pattern of Kansas politics. The Republicans are dominant and therefore win most state-wide elections. But the Democrats are sufficiently numerous so that they are able to win election victories when a relatively small percentage of Republicans reject one or more of their party's nominees. This happens periodically. The Democrats captured the gubernatorial office in 1882, 1912, 1922, 1930, 1936, 1956 and 1958. In each of these elections some short term influence momentarily upset the balance of power. The nature of these influences has varied. In 1882 it was dissatisfaction with the incumbent Republican governor's preoccupation with the fight for prohibition and his aspiration for a third term. In 1912 it was the split between Bull-Moosers and Standpatters. In 1922 it was a severe agricultural depression. In 1930 it was a combination of a recession and the uncompromising personality of the incumbent Republican governor who was defeated in his own primary in a bid to be renominated for a second term. In 1936 it was the depression. In 1956 it was the schism in the Republican Party between pro-Hall and anti-Hall factions. In 1958 it appeared to have been satisfaction with the incumbent Democratic governor's conservative administration plus generally unsettled farm conditions. Whatever the short term influences may be, Democrats in Kansas win only with the help of defecting Republican voters. President Johnson received such help in the 1964 presidential election in Kansas.

This historic pattern is not likely to change unless and until the social and economic character of Kansas undergoes a major transformation. These changes are occurring in other states, but in the heartland of America nothing is happening that now promises significant alteration in the political balance of power.

FOOTNOTES

[1] There are twelve precincts in Wichita which are predominantly, although not exclusively, Negro. The Johnson-Humphrey ticket received 89 per cent of the total presidential vote in these precincts.

The defection of Republican identifiers among negro voters had been predicted on the basis of a poll conducted by the *Kansas City Star* in the Kansas City area. Alvin McCoy, veteran member of the *Star's* staff, had reported that interviewers had failed to find any Negroes who would say that they would vote for Senator Goldwater.

The 1964 Presidential Election In Arkansas

GEORGE C. ROBERTS

University of Arkansas

While the 1964 presidential campaign may not have been particularly exciting in Arkansas, the election outcome was interesting insomuch as Arkansas did not follow the Republican trend of the deep South. The *Arkansas Gazette* was moved to proclaim, "We have never been prouder of 'the Democracy' in Arkansas than for its refusal to be driven to any contrary conclusion in this election."[1]

An important phase of the 1964 presidential election in Arkansas began with the selection of delegates to the parties' national conventions. Arkansas Republicans had twelve votes at their convention, compared to sixteen in 1960, and selected twelve delegates and twelve alternates. Perhaps as a sign of a newer Republican Party, only two of the 1960 delegates served as a delegate or alternate in 1964. The chairman of the delegation was Winthrop Rockefeller, Republican candidate for Governor, newcomer to Arkansas and to politics, and National Committeeman since 1961.[2] The party's State Committee, meeting on May 21, selected four at-large delegates and alternates while ratifying the two delegates and alternates chosen the previous week by party committees in each of four congressional districts. This activity was marked by and preceded by factional feuding between Rockefeller and State Chairman William Spicer, spokesman of the Old Guard. Rockefeller delegates were selected from the Third Congressional District by a 15-5 vote in a Fayetteville session after the presiding officer had been overruled on a procedural matter.[3] Before the State Committee met, Spicer, in a confidential memorandum to selected party leaders, noted that Republican support for Governor Orval Faubus, Rockefeller's general election opponent, was possible.[4] However, Rockefeller forces prevailed at the meeting and the State Committee instructed the delegates to nominate Rockefeller as a favorite-son candidate, in spite of sentiment among the delegates for the nomination of Senator Barry Goldwater.[5] Spicer became the first State Chairman not to go as a delegate to the National Convention.[6]

At San Francisco Rockefeller canceled plans for his nomination because it would have followed the nomination of his brother, Nelson. Before Goldwater's nomination was made unanimous Arkansas delegates cast nine votes for Senator Goldwater, two for Governor William Scranton, one for Governor Nelson Rockefeller, leaving Goldwater without the solid support he had in most southern delegations.[7]

Arkansas Democrats had thirty-two votes at their 1964 National Convention, where they had held twenty-seven votes in 1960. They had been permitted fifty-one delegates in 1960, and were permitted fifty-four in 1964, twenty-six alternates in 1960, thirty in 1964. Tom Harper, National Committeeman, served as delegation chairman, as he had in 1960. Of the fifty-one 1960 delegates fifteen served as 1964 delegates, while four more were 1964 alternates, making for more continuity than in the Republican group. Governor Faubus was not a delegate to either convention, Congressman Oren Harris served in both, and Senators Jack McClellan and William Fulbright only in 1964.[8] The selection of delegates by the Democratic State Committee lacked the factionalism of the Republicans.

At Atlantic City the Arkansas delegation backed the compromise plan for seating Mississippi delegates, and Fulbright seconded Senator Hubert Humphrey's nomination for Vice-President. Arkansas delegates did not walk out of the Convention in sympathy with Mississippi delegates, but six delegates, including three Faubus advisors, were reportedly unhappy. Governor Faubus expressed fear that if Arkansas delegates left the hall their places would be taken by a group led by Mrs. Daisy Bates, a spokesman for the NAACP in Arkansas.[9]

The lateness of the Democratic National Convention placed the nomination phase close to the general election campaign. But indeed the response of Arkansas Democrats and Republicans to their party presidential nominee was related to the organization of campagin efforts and the activitiy that would follow.

In August it became known that John Greiner, Goldwater's regional manager for the South, had greatly aided Winthrop Rockefeller on the eve of his State Committee struggle with Chairman Spicer, an enthusiastic backer of Goldwater for the presidential nomination. In effect, Greiner had pledged support to Rockefeller in his gubernatorial race, and had approved an uncommitted delegation to San Francisco. In June two officials of the Arkansas draft-Goldwater movement lost their jobs. Finally Spicer was replaced as State Chairman. Then Republican National Chairman Dean Burch asked Rockefeller to help him select leaders for the Goldwater campaign organization in Arkansas.[10] In September, when Goldwater spoke in Memphis, Rockefeller crossed the Mississippi to sit on the speaker's platform and hear praise from Goldwater.[11] The next week Rockefeller praised Goldwater in New Mexico and earlier had told Arkansans, "I can subscribe to Goldwater's philosophies more easily than Faubus can. . . . It will be easy to see if Faubus espouses Mr. Goldwater or whether he recognizes his oath to the Democratic Party."[12] But in a sense Rockefeller and Goldwater campaign organizations went separate ways, and while some Goldwater literature was available at Rockefeller headquarters, the Rockefeller newspaper, the *W R Campaigner,* gave Goldwater no mention, and Rockefeller said little about Goldwater on the stump.[13] As columnist Roy Reed noted in the *Gazette* at the close of the campaign, "Rockefeller has had more to say in praise of Goldwater than Faubus has in praise of Johnson, but neither man has been noticeably eager to ride the coattails of the national leader."[14] In January, 1965, Rowland Evans and Robert Novak wrote in the *New York Herald-Tribune* (Rockefeller denying) that had Dean Burch not agreed to step down as National Chairman when he did, Rockefeller, with approval of the Republican State Committee, would have exposed tactics employed by Goldwater leaders in Arkansas during the campaign. These tactics, such as appointment of a former Faubus appointee to state office as co-chairman of Arkansas Citizens for Goldwater, allegedly weakened Rockefeller's chances to defeat Faubus.[15] But then, Rockefeller was supposed to have approved this appointment.

At the fall Republican State Convention it was agreed to turn $3,000 in state party funds over to the Goldwater campaign organization.[16] With much fanfare the Arkansas Goldwater for President Committee announced the opening of state headquarters in Little Rock on September 17. Yet local efforts lagged and were separated from Rockefeller efforts. In Washington County, for instance, the first Goldwater headquarters did not open until later, and a county seat headquarters did not open until October 24. Eventually Goldwater and Rockefeller headquarters were about equal in number, and 10,000 Goldwater volunteers were reported, but Rockefeller organization was more vigorous.[17] Goldwater supporters may have thought too much party effort went into Rockefeller's campaign, but Goldwater Republicans did not show the type of enthusiasm in the general election campaign they had shown months before when they worked towards Goldwater's nomination. Of course, some local party efforts, directed primarily toward Rockefeller's candidacy, aided Goldwater. When Washington County Young Republicans used one hundred volunteers to contact 8,000 voters[18] such activity could but help all Republican candidates, although some of the volunteers wanting to aid Rockefeller would never admit this. Goldwater headquarter practices of charging for campaign materials (not limited to Arkansas and true also of the pre-convention period), seemed particularly inept. Thus when a Rockefeller headquarters distributed Goldwater material they set a price on it because they had paid for it.

At the state level, on the other hand, during the campaign, newspaper advertisements for Goldwater were paid for by the Republican State Committee. As mentioned above, a Goldwater for President Committee, with Dabbs Sullivan Jr. as chairman, was formed, as well as a Citizens for Goldwater Committee, with co-chairmen W. R. Smith and L. C. B. Young. An Arkansas for Goldwater Committee was headed by one of the Goldwater leaders forced out of office in June, E. E. Barber Jr., and finally Arkansas Mothers for a Moral America was organized.[19]

As noted above, Goldwater forces recruited a Faubus political appointee as a Citizens Committee co-chairman. Also Associate Justice Jim Johnson of the Arkansas Supreme Court, elected as a Democrat, campaigned with strong endorsements of Goldwater. Generally however more Arkansas Democratic leaders were attracted to Rockefeller's candidacy. They were perhaps conservative enough to accept Goldwater's ideology, but their support of his candidacy was not apparent. Ben T. Laney, a former Governor and Dixiecrat of 1948, who managed Rockefeller's rice farms, aided Rockefeller's campaign.[20] Joe Hardin, a conservative Faubus primary election opponent of 1960 appeared at a Rockefeller rally, but also at a Democratic rally "to cheer Lyndon Johnson."[21] Vernon Whitten, a conservative opponent of Faubus in the 1962 primary election organized Independent Citizens for Rockefeller. He explained that he was not a Republican, but was not for Faubus. He said, "I consider the national Democratic administration now too liberal and so I can't call myself a national Democrat," and cited Faubus's endorsement of the Johnson-Humphrey ticket as one reason for his action.[22] It is interesting that these potential presidential Republicans were most active in support of the Republican gubernatorial candidate.

In August, 1964, it was not clear as to what efforts would be made in Arkansas for the Democratic presidential candidate. There were Arkansans who called themselves national Democrats, but also those who called themselves state Democrats. Some national Democrats remembered with uneasiness the 1960 presidential campaign in Arkansas. It began with Governor Faubus, Senator Fulbright, and Congressman Oren Harris appearing with Senator Jack Kennedy at a Texarkana rally, and with state party leaders promising that a campaign organization would be active for the first time since 1928 because one was needed. The leaders were taken seriously by some Young Democrats who opened a Kennedy headquarters in Little Rock. However, it was soon closed on orders from "high party officials."[23] Senator Fulbright, facing an election in 1962, was not active in the campaign. At the last minute a newspaper advertisement informed the public that a party meeting, upon Senator McClellan's motion, had informed Senator Kennedy that Arkansas was with him.[24] Yet no real local effort was made to aid Kennedy. Democrats were not organized locally for the gubernatorial campaign as they would be in 1962, and a handful of college Kennedy-Johnson Clubs carried the burden. They received almost no assistance from the local party organizations and leaders. Their material came from national party offices or from local labor unions.

Prior to the convening of the Democratic National Convention in 1964 Governor Faubus foresaw reaction to the national administration because of the 1964 Civil Rights Act, and noted the possibility of a turnover. He said he preferred a change in view, not in personality.[25] The writer spoke with Arkansas politicians who hinted of a formal Goldwater-Faubus alliance in east Arkansas. The Governor was saying that as of August 11, Goldwater would probably carry Arkansas, and a few days later met with the Governors of four other southern states in closed session to discuss convention strategy, particularly if the regular Mississippi delegation were not seated.[26] Only six of twenty-six National Convention delegates questioned would flatly predict a Johnson victory in Arkansas.

In 1962, when Democrats felt obliged to open a state campaign headquarters for the first time in a number of years and established county party headquarters, both Faubus and Fulbright faced an election with Republican opponents. Faubus could say that Arkansas Democrats should "overcome the mistakes of the national Administration,"[27] but the Democratic "top team" approach smothered individual candidate policy differences within the State by stressing Faubus's popularity, Washington respect for Fulbright, and power wielded by a four-chairmen congressional delegation. But could the "top team" approach appeal to Arkansas Democrats in 1964 when an external candidate for President was part of the political situation? In effect, the "top team" approach was expanded for 1964 purposes and there emerged the "precinct to presidency" concept, formally endorsed by party and interest groups, and repeated by individual Democrats at the grass roots.[28] President Lyndon Johnson, Arkansas's neighbor, became part of the "top team," and Democrats argued that he could help the Arkansas delegation secure more blessings for Arkansas. But the possibility of such a development depended heavily on the personal reaction of Governor Faubus to Johnson's candidacy and attention must now be focused on the Governor's role.

Speculation about a Faubus endorsement of Senator Goldwater ended on September 12, when the Governor announced, "I join . . . in support of the Democratic nominees and the Democratic ticket," and said he would be with President Johnson when he visited Arkansas later in the month. Along with this first public endorsement of the national ticket came knowledge that Senator Hubert Humphrey could appear in Arkansas at Faubus's invitation.[29] The next day Faubus explained that he had no choice but to support all party nominees of the Democratic Party under state party rules because he was a candidate, noting further, "I don't think that anything I say or anything that Mr. Rockefeller says will affect to any appreciable degree the outcome of the national election." He argued that the National Democratic platform represented a concensus and was a good platform and that the Democratic Party represented the peoples' interests better than the Republican Party.[30] Immediately the Little Rock Capital Citizens Council criticized Faubus and the *Gazette* reported a "backlash" against him for his Johnson endorsement. Rockefeller hoped for votes from those upset by the endorsement, asserting "his espousing the liberal cause is something they won't stand still for."[31]

The Governor announced through his own newspaper, the *Arkansas Statesman*, that he would see President Johnson in

Texarkana because the appearance was non-political and because
he had been invited along with the Governors of Louisiana, Texas,
and Oklahoma.[32] When the President appeared there on September
25, Faubus rode in the presidential car, made remarks at the
Kennedy memorial dedication, and played the role of a good
host.[33] In October Mrs. Faubus would serve as hostess to Mrs.
Johnson on her visit to Arkansas. A note of discord was sounded
when two men claimed they were given Goldwater literature at
a Faubus headquarters in Little Rock, but the headquarters denied
the story.[34] During the campaign, the *Arkansas Statesman*, Faubus's
weekly newspaper, reported campaign appearances of Johnson
and Humphrey, but thereafter ignored the national campaign,
stressing instead the state campaign. There were editorials, mostly
reprinted from other sources, critical of some of the policies associated with the Johnson Administration, such as Medicare.[35]

Whatever motives Governor Faubus may have had for his
Johnson endorsement, he had little to gain politically therefrom
in Arkansas for the moment. As noted above, Rockefeller moved
to gain votes from the action, and it was not enough to cause all
national Democrats to vote for Faubus. Certainly a post-election
statement from an anti-Faubus race relations group to the effect
that Faubus rode back into office on Johnson's "coattails" was not
supported by the returns which showed that Faubus polled 23,292
more votes than Johnson.

Another boost to the Johnson cause came in the closing days
of the campaign when Faubus spokesmen were sent to eastern
Arkansas to urge county leaders to hold their counties for Johnson.
Legislators and others who had publically declared support for
Goldwater were changing their endorsements.[36] But the early
Faubus endorsement was a psychological shot to Arkansas Demo-
crats who wanted to aid their national ticket. Organization and a
fairly high level of party unity followed immediately.

The Democratic State Convention was held within a week of
the Faubus endorsement. Unity was its theme, Hubert Humphrey
its featured speaker, and several state spokesmen asked for national ticket support. Tom Harper, National Committeeman, got
immediate pledges for $25,000 to support the national ticket from
members of the Legislature and state boards, many of whom had
influenced the Faubus endorsement.[37] Before September ended,
Jack Files, Young Democratic National Committeeman and a
former secretary to Congressman Wilbur Mills, was named full-

time campaign director for the Arkansas Democratic Campaign Committee. Its headquarters was a focal point for all Democratic nominees, but the state party gave it the national ticket as its main concern and separate Faubus headquarters were established.[38] A Young People for Johnson group worked through this office. A Young Citizens for Johnson-Humphrey group was controlled by national and state Young Democratic bodies, while Young Democratic Voters was set up by the state group. Supposedly at the suggestion of Congressman Mills, Citizens for Johnson-Humphrey was also organized. Lee Williams, as assistant to Senator Fulbright, actually coordinated efforts for the national ticket through this office, probably at the President's request. Rural Americans for Johnson-Humphrey actively sponsored newspaper advertisements in the state. Also, a Students for Johnson-Humphrey group, headed by Jack Coleman, President of the University of Arkansas Young Democrats Club, had state headquarters in Fayetteville. This was probably the only group appointed free of state party control, and factional opponents lessened its impact on the campaign.[39]

It is likely that one reason so many groups were formed to help the national ticket was because several politicians, especially younger leaders, anticipated a post-Faubus era and wanted to attract the attention of fellow Democrats. They wanted it known in later years that they had been loyal and had helped shape the Johnson victory of 1964. In view of the personal rivalries exhibited it is amazing that Johnson's candidacy wasn't hindered rather than helped by such group activity. At any rate the situation was remarkably different from 1960 when there were no comparable groups actively supporting Kennedy, and certainly in 1964 Democrats had enough organization to overshadow Goldwater organization. Roy Reed, *Gazette* columnist, reported it as a case of 1,000 professional Johnson volunteers and 10,000 dedicated Goldwater amateurs.[40]

Senator McClellan thought in July that the Republican Party had nominated "its best and strongest man" for the Presidency, and without endorsing Johnson, noted he was a Democrat.[41] On October 12, he endorsed Johnson's candidacy by saying he would support all levels of the ticket.[42] Finally his most lavish compliment was paid at the LBJ Ranch where he called Johnson "a great President," and called for his election.[43]

Compared to 1960, Senator Fulbright conducted an active 1964 campaign for President Johnson. His statements concerning Senator Goldwater's foreign policy concepts were distributed by the Democratic National Committee and released for Arkansas consumption through the state campaign headquarters.[44] Fulbright stumped Arkansas and other states in support of the President. In a two and one-half week period he planned six major speeches in Arkansas and three elsewhere.[45]

For the first time since the days of Franklin Roosevelt Arkansas's congressional delegation gave "unqualified support" to the presidential nominee, and this included the support of Delta Congressman E. C. Gathings, previously cool to the national Democrats, who urged his constituents to go with him in support of Lyndon Johnson.[46]

Johnson's campaign received support also from interest groups and their spokesmen. The state AFL-CIO COPE convention endorsed all Democratic nominees, the first support for Faubus since 1954.[47] Labor support for Johnson was characterized as extensive and effective, but not overly noticeable.[48] Harry L. Oswald, general manager of the Arkansas State Electric Cooperative, Inc., was named southern regional coordinator of Rural Americans for Johnson-Humphrey, a group very active at the state level in Arkansas. Region Eight of the National Electric Cooperative Association helped invite Humphrey to Arkansas, and he addressed their Hot Springs convention. Individuals associated with the electrical cooperative movement in Arkansas helped arrange Mrs. Johnson's visit to Little Rock.[49] Forrest Rozzell, executive secretary of the Arkansas Education Association, served as a member of the Arkansas Citizens for Johnson-Humphrey Committee and issued statements critical of Goldwater's views on education.[50]

Arkansas Republicans were probably too concerned with Winthrop Rockefeller's race to furnish significant support for Johnson through a citizens-type group, but a Democrats for Rockefeller groups' leader claimed to be a national Democrat for Johnson, opposed to Faubus because he was not a national party supporter.

With these political endorsements and such a state level organizational structure was there enough party unity in Arkansas to aid the national ticket? Faubus's Johnson endorsement did not mean he was campaigning for Johnson. He was concerned with his own campaign and did not desire to antagonize Goldwater voters willing to support his candidacy. When Arkansas Democrats held a $10-a-box supper rally in Little Rock on October 26, the Gover-

nor was campaigning elsewhere, and columnist Roy Reed reported
that 1,700 Democrats were not all there to cheer the same heroes.
The overlap was not complete between Johnson and Faubus
Democrats. Senator Fulbright brought cheers for the President,
Senator McClellan cheers for the Governor, while other speakers
were able to mention names all could cheer.[51]

The State Committee publication, *Democratic News,* ignored the
national campaign,[52] and at the state level campaign organization
for the state ticket was separate from that for the national ticket
as has been noted. Yet at the county level Faubus and Johnson
forces, when not one and the same, developed a cooperative
organization which made the Goldwater-Rockefeller organization
split look like warfare. It was symbolic that at the Little Rock
Arkansas Livestock Exhibition the Faubus and Johnson literature
distributors used the same booth, while the Goldwater and Rockefeller booths were separate.[53] The Faubus campaign bulletin listed
local Faubus headquarters, but the address was often the same for
groups working for President Johnson.[54]

The organization set-up in Fayetteville, Washington County will
illustrate organizational cooperation. In 1960 Democrats had no
campaign headquarters there. In 1962 the Faubus primary election
headquarters became general election headquarters for Faubus,
Fulbright, the congressional nominee, and local candidates. In
1964 campaign workers for national, state, and local offices were
housed in the same roomy quarters. Some division of effort was
maintained, although literature was mixed and window posters
heralded all-level candidates. One corner, occupied by county committee workers, concentrated on the county, legislative, and state
candidates.[55] Contributions made in this corner brought letters of
thanks from the Governor's Office. Washington County Young
Democrats occupied another corner and their literature and fund-
raising activities primarily benefited Johnson and the congressional
candidate. Upstairs there were facilities for the state offices of
Students for Johnson-Humphrey. When it became necessary to
arrange for political caravans, rallies, and voter canvassing all of
these elements were able to assist the general campaign effort without much friction. The writer spent considerable time in the headquarters without hearing any disputes between Johnson and
Faubus over money, buttons, pamphlets, or personalities. In a
sense there was an ideological gulf between the county committee
people and the Young Democrats, but it did not destroy organiza-

tional effectiveness. Actually, the regulars did not know much about conducting a general election campaign since they usually felt no need to do so. The Young Democrats had energy for this task, and the regulars assisted their efforts for the national ticket with money. Thus the headquarters groups coalesced for the campaign.

A summary of organizational efforts indicates that there were several important party and interest groups active state-wide in support of the Johnson-Humphrey ticket. In some cases, national party groups preferred contact with local party workers and no state organization. Material of Scientists and Engineers for Johnson-Humphrey was mailed locally and funds solicited locally. The Democratic National Committee's Operation Support for Johnson-Humphrey program would work best in Arkansas if locally organized, its regional coordinator felt, although in thirty-seven states organization at the state level was preferred.[56] If state groups had no local units, they were apt to deal with the local party head-quarters, often called "Faubus Headquarters," and usually sponsored by the county party officials. It was cooperative effort at the local level which made Democratic victory easier.[57] This effort was missing in 1960, along with any significant state effort, but in 1964 it was most noticeable alongside an ineffective local Goldwater effort and lack of local Goldwater-Rockefeller headquarters co-operation.

In April, 1962, Congressman William Miller, Chairman of the Republican National Committee, was featured speaker at a tent rally of revivified Arkansas Republicanism in Fayetteville, and Senator Barry Goldwater spoke in Little Rock as part of the effort to unseat Senator William Fulbright. However, during the 1964 presidential campaign neither Republican campaigned in Arkansas. Goldwater spoke in Memphis and expressed hope of making several Arkansas appearances later.[58] As events unfolded Republicans attracted as their only important speakers Senator J. Strom Thurmond of South Carolina and Texas Senator John Tower. Tower's address to a $50-a-plate Goldwater for President dinner was sponsored by Citizens for Goldwater.[59]

The Johnson-Humphrey team, on the other hand, was in Arkansas three times. Senator Hubert Humphrey came first on September 18, as noted above at the invitation of Governor Faubus and electrical cooperative interests. His first speech was to 2,500 in Hot Springs National Park and was keyed to rural electrification. He was introduced by Senator Fulbright and accompanied by Congressman Harris. He then proceeded by caravan to Little Rock where he addressed a similarly sized crowd assembled for the Democratic State Convention. There he stressed party unity, praised the President, and attacked Goldwater for not voting in the Senate to aid the South. Governor Faubus was praised for assistance to rural electrification and economic and farm improvement. Faubus was absent from both Humphrey speeches with a respiratory ailment which hospitalized him and took him out of the campaign for several days, and Mrs. Faubus substituted for him at the Convention.[60]

President and Mrs. Johnson followed a week later. Coming from an El Paso meeting with Mexican President Adolfo Lopez Mateos and an Oklahoma dam dedication the President stood on the state line at Texarkana, where President Kennedy had stood in 1960, to dedicate a Kennedy memorial with a "non-political" speech. Some 2,500 people had greeted the President at the airport, and possibly 45,000 heard the late dedication speech, fewer than had heard Kennedy in 1960. Perhaps Negroes comprised a fifth of the crowd, which heard remarks on civil rights, extremism, voices of despair, minimum wage laws, and the Test Ban Treaty. Turning to his host, Governor Faubus, the President quoted Robert E. Lee, "Abandon all these local animosities—and make your sons Americans."[61]

On October 24, the President spoke in Memphis, but Arkansas Democrats did not count this speech as part of their campaign effort. But Mrs. Johnson was warmly greeted on October 27, when she spoke at a Fort Smith dedication of a historical site to 5,000 people. The First Lady was escorted by Congressman J. W. Trimble and accompanied by Senator and Mrs. Fulbright, Mrs. Faubus and the wives of several Cabinet members. Mrs. Johnson then proceeded to Little Rock for an appearance in MacArthur Park where she was introduced by Senator McClellan.[62]

With such organizational establishments and candidate activities what strategy was followed by each party in regard to issues raised in the campaign? Of course, at some point in the campaign, or somewhere, most of the issues raised in the presidential campaign nationally would be raised in Arkansas. The same kind of Campaign pamphlets distributed by the Democratic National Committee or its subsidiary groups reached Arkansas that went elsewhere, and covered a variety of issues. While Senator Fulbright was a national spokesman on foreign policy matters, in Arkansas domestic issues were also discussed. An examination of literature prepared by Washington County Young Democrats, a group primarily active in support of the national ticket, stressed Johnson and Goldwater reaction to such matters as peace, bomb testing, tax cuts, poverty, social security, employment, small business, agriculture, and rural electrification.[63]

Yet if Democratic publicity is viewed at the state level, and particularly engineered by state party spokesman and the State Democratic Campaign Committee, it becomes evident that the presidential election campaign was conducted similarly to the 1962 campaign when state officials and national legislative officials were elected. The Democratic organization stressed the same issues in both campaigns. One approach, which could be called the populist-depression-prosperity approach, was in great part an appeal to a rural Arkansas (a majority of the state's population was still rural in 1960). State Chairman Catlett spoke of the kind of freedom Goldwater promoted as being that which "kept Arkansas in economic bondage to the Eastern money interests for decades."[64] A pamphlet distributed by Washington County Rural Americans for Johnson-Humphrey was entitled *Remember The Depression?* Goldwater's positions on farm subsidy programs, rural electrification, and the Tennessee Valley Authority were second, while Arkansas prosperity was praised.[65] To accentuate this rural depression approach Rural Americans for Johnson-Humphrey sponsored a "Whippoorwill Pea" dinner at which Democrats in old-fashioned dress ate peas, turnips, sow belly, and cornbread by kerosene lamp light and talked of the good old (Republican) days.

Somewhat related to the rural approach was stress given Goldwater's Senate votes against the Arkansas River navigation project. The State Democratic Campaign Committee pointed out that $113,000,000, more than for any other state, had been appropriated by Congress in 1964 for Arkansas water programs, but that Goldwater favored water projects for Arizona only.[66] Then followed the top team argument. Arkansas River development funds could be guaranteed only by keeping a seniority-laden congressional delegation in Washington where it could work with a Democratic President who would support its goals.

Probably one reason this populist-depression-prosperity-top team approach was used for presidential campaign purposes was because it complemented Governor Faubus's state campaign. Advertisements, supposedly concerned with the congressional delegation, included the Governor as part of the "top team." Faubus campaign speeches related the Rockefeller family to the price paid for kerosene when Faubus was a boy. The Governor told the state AFL-CIO, "It has been my observation that corporations have little, if any, conscience."[67] He charged that Rockefeller had boasted in a California speech that he could hire workers in Arkansas for fifty cents an hour.[68] The liberal bread and butter approach to welfare and educational programs figured in Faubus's campaign. After the election the Governor remarked, "Goldwater's position on Social Security, the Arkansas River development program, on rural electrification and other programs such as unemployment insurance, alarmed many. . . ."[69]

Democratic concentration on such matters as the Arkansas River project and farm problems put Arkansas Republicans on the defensive in the presidential campaign. A Goldwater spokesman admitted that Goldwater counted on heavy support in southeastern and eastern Arkansas, and charged that farmers were misinformed on Goldwater's farm views.[70] The *Gazette* editorially noted that Robert E. Lee Wilson III, the finance chairman of the Arkansas for Goldwater group, although critical of federal intervention in private affairs, headed a company which in 1959 secured over $716,000 in governmental loans on rice, soybeans, and cotton.[71] At the end of the campaign Arkansas Goldwater headquarters made public a telegram in which Senator Goldwater "confirmed his support" of Arkansas River projects already begun on the grounds that congressional commitments should be honored.[72] Goldwater's "actual views" on social security were presented.[73]

Moving from the defensive, the Goldwater for President group sponsored full-page newspaper endorsements of Goldwater's candidacy by former President Dwight Eisenhower,[74] a strange tactic in view of Eisenhower's association with Little Rock in 1957. A Citizens for Goldwater group featured advertisements concerned with Americans for Democratic Action, socialism, Hubert Humphrey, and one-world government.[75] After the arrest of presidential assistant Walter Jenkins on a morals charge "an open letter to the people of Arkansas" paid for by Dabbs Sullivan Jr., chairman of the Goldwater for President Committee, argued that in their work President Johnson and Jenkins had shared a relationship as close as that in marriage, and that the President could not properly evaluate his associates, was trying to cover up their actions, or had a moral code radically different from most Americans.[76]

Did the race issue figure prominently in the campaign? In September Governor Faubus remarked on racial demonstrations, "The first time they lay down in the streets to block the traffic of a legitimate business operation, they're going to get run over. And if no one else will do it, I'll get in a truck and do it myself."[77] Later Faubus complained that attempts by a former Rockefeller employee to purchase poll tax receipts in Pulaski County for Negro voters amounted to "wholesale fraud."[78] Just before the election a Republican worker was seen emerging from a Goldwater headquarters in Little Rock and attaching to windshields a Johnson brochure that bore the address of the Democratic National Committee. It carried pictures of Johnson with various Negro leaders. Republicans sponsored a telecast in which Associate Justice Jim Johnson of the Arkansas Supreme Court endorsed Goldwater as an opponent of the "damnable" 1964 Civil Rights Act.[79] But national Democrats took the Negro vote for granted insofar as the presidential vote was concerned, and felt that opposition to Goldwater's farm policies would outweigh the race issue in east Arkansas.[80] Republicans interested in Rockefeller's campaign did not want the race issue stressed particularly, feeling that their candidate was vulnerable on the question.

Although this was not the case during the whole campaign, a look at the political advertisements and editorial comments in the *Arkansas Gazette* on the Sunday before the election indicates little interest at all in national issues and candidates since almost all of these sections dealt with state and local campaigns.[81]

The two daily newspapers of overwhelming circulation[82] in the state, the *Arkansas Gazette* and the *Arkansas Democrat*, both published in Little Rock, both editorially endorsed the national Democratic ticket. The *Gazette* did so on September 13, and likewise editorially supported the general policies of the Johnson Administration. On the other hand Johnson policies were not always acceptable to the *Democrat*. It did not endorse Johnson until October 31, in an editorial which continually balanced the candidates, finally concluding that Johnson was a leader who got things done, and that his election would give Arkansas a stronger voice in Washington.

Unfortunately there were no public polls to measure voter sentiment in Arkansas during the campaign. Goldwater supporters cited a private poll showing an even situation by election time, while Democrats quoted a poll giving Johnson sixty per cent of the vote.[83] Johnson actually polled about fifty-six per cent of the total votes cast.

Since the payment of a poll tax as a prerequisite for voting for federal officials had been abolished by amendment of the United States Constitution, free poll tax receipts were issued for those who wished them, as the poll tax system was the closest thing Arkansas had to a voter registration system.[84] Holders of these free receipts could not vote for state officials unless they possessed the one dollar receipt. Thus two types of ballots were used.

The 1960 Arkansas ballot, of the office-block type, listed only presidential elector candidates, not the names of presidential candidates, but the 1964 ballot, still the office-block type, reversed this situation. The Secretary of State issued confusing instructions to local officials so that some Arkansas ballots grouped a party's presidential and vice-presidential candidates while others separated them. This produced additionally some voter confusion, and although of course votes were actually cast for electors, Johnson and Goldwater polled more popular votes than Humphrey and Miller. Election officials in Fayetteville told the writer that some ballots were invalidated when voters marked for the Democratic or Republican candidate for President and then for the National States Rights candidate, probably thinking they were simply endorsing the "states rights" concept. For the first time many Arkansas voted in voting booths, constructed of cardboard and essentially furnished by Republicans, who for several years had complained of voting irregularities.

At one point in the campaign the Associated Press spoke of "unprecedented interest" in the presidential contest in Arkansas, an interest not so noticeable to those acquainted with genuine two-party politics.[85] Yet the 560,426 votes cast in the presidential race, compared to 428,509 cast in 1960, were the most votes cast in any of the presidential races beginning with 1948. Still 31,687 more votes were cast in the gubernatorial contest, while in 1960 the presidential race had attracted 6,524 more voters. Also, Arkansas had only 43 per cent of its population of voting age participating in the presidential race, and the national figure was 60.6 per cent. Only six states and the District of Columbia ranked lower.[86] The State Auditor reported that 715,528 poll tax receipts were purchased in 1964 and 2,009 free receipts were issued. He estimated that 56 per cent of those purchasing receipts were male, and that about two-thirds of those of voting age had done so. Only 603,795 receipts had been issued in 1960.[87] In 1964, 78.1 per cent of those thus eligible to vote had cast presidential ballots.

President Lyndon Johnson, carrying sixty-five of seventy-five counties, received 314,197 of 560,426 votes cast in the 1964 election in Arkansas; Senator Barry Goldwater received 243,264 votes; and John Kasper, National States Rights candidate, received 2,965 votes.[88] Johnson polled 56.4 per cent of the two-party vote, with a plurality of 70,933 over Goldwater, and trailed Governor Faubus by 23,292 votes. In 1960 Kennedy's plurality over Nixon had been 30,541, he trailed Faubus by 77,015, and he polled 53.8 per cent of the two-party vote. However, Kennedy's percentage of the total vote was only 50.2, since the National States Rights Party with Orval Faubus as candidate received 6.7 per cent of the total vote. Johnson's 314,197 votes were the most any Democratic presidential candidate had received in Arkansas in the 1948-1964 period, his plurality over his Republican opponent was exceeded only by Harry Truman in 1948, and his percentage of the two-party vote was topped only by Truman. Truman also received a greater percentage of the total votes cast than did Johnson, but more votes were cast in 1964 than in any other election. (See Table I).

Before the 1964 presidential election political observers advanced several hypotheses concerning the expected Goldwater vote pattern. One proposition was that Goldwater would run well where William J. Bryan had in 1896. But Bryan lost only two Arkansas counties to McKinley and Goldwater carried only ten counties.[89] Another speculation was that Goldwater would do better than Nixon in the South, with race the prime factor, and therefore Goldwater would carry much of the Delta in eastern and southeastern Arkansas. However, of the ten counties Goldwater carried, only one could properly be called a Delta county, Arkansas, noted for high income rice production. Three more Goldwater counties were in the northwestern traditional Republican hill region. Another, Sebastian, was in hill country, was urban, and had been noted for rightist political activity. The other five Goldwater counties in southern Arkansas could best be compared to the sandy, pine tree, upper coastal counties of the Atlantic Seaboard.[90] If the twenty-four counties in which Goldwater polled 45 per cent or more of the vote are considered, only five could properly be called Delta Counties. In a geographical, agricultural production

TABLE 1

VOTE IN ARKANSAS PRESIDENTIAL ELECTIONS

1948-1964

Election	Vote Total	Democratic Vote	Republican Vote	Other Vote	Democratic-Republican Plurality	Dem. Percent of Two-Party Vote	Dem. Percent of Total Vote
1948	242,475	149,659	50,959	41,857[a]	98,700	74.6	62.2
1952	404,800	226,300	177,155	1,345	49,145	56.1	55.9
1956	406,572	213,277	186,287	7,008	26,990	53.4	52.5
1960	428,509	215,049	184,508	28,952[b]	30,541	53.8	50.2
1964	560,426	314,197	243,264	2,965	70,933	56.4	56.1

[a] Mostly States Rights.
[b] All National States Rights.

sense Arkansas did not join the deep South. Faubus endorsement of Johnson, machine county voting (including control of the Negro vote), and farm issues probably accounted for this difference.

A comparison of Goldwater counties to Johnson counties reveals that 40 per cent of the ten Goldwater counties were more Dixiecrat than the state in 1948, and 42 per cent of the sixty-five Johnson counties were, but 50 per cent of the Goldwater counties had a heavier non-white population than the state in 1960, this being true of only 38 per cent of the Johnson counties.[91] Compared to the state in 1960, 30 per cent of the Goldwater counties were more urban, only 17 per cent of the Johnson counties were. Considering the percentage of median family incomes under $3,000 in 1959, 40 per cent of the Goldwater counties were poorer than the state, but 86 per cent of the Johnson counties were. All the Goldwater counties lost population between 1950 and 1960, half of them at a rate greater than the state.

A better analysis of the statewide vote can be made by considering the twenty-four counties in which Goldwater got at least 45 per cent of the two-party vote.[92] In terms of being more Dixiecrat than the state in 1948, these Goldwater-oriented counties register 62 per cent, the others 31 percent. Compared to the state, 62 per cent of the Goldwater counties had a heavier non-white population, only 29 per cent of the other counties did. Also 29 per cent of the Goldwater counties were more urban than the state, 14 per cent of the other counties were. Included in this expanded Goldwater category was Pulaski County (Little Rock), the state's most populated county (242,980 population in 1960, the next county having 81,373). Johnson polled only 51.4 per cent of the two-party vote in Pulaski. In terms of median family income, 62 per cent of the Goldwater counties were poorer than the state, but 88 per cent of the other counties were. Thus the 45 per cent or more Goldwater-oriented counties showed about twice the tendency to be more Dixiecrat, more non-white, and more urban than the whole state. However, the other counties tended to be poorer than the state to a greater extent than the Goldwater-oriented counties.

Senator Goldwater and Winthrop Rockefeller both carried ten Arkansas counties in 1964, but only four counties cast majorities for both candidates at the same time. Three of these were northwestern hill counties, the fourth, Sebastian, urban as well. Goldwater carried six southern counties which Rockefeller did not, and Rockefeller carried three rural hill and three urban counties which Goldwater did not.[93]

The *New York Times* reported after the election that Rockefeller did best in Johnson counties, a report undoubtedly based on Arkansas press information.[94] In some voting areas Johnson and Rockefeller polled about the same percentage of the two-party vote, as shown below, but the *Times* report was not an accurate picture of the whole state. Rockefeller carried 40 per cent of the Goldwater counties, only 9 per cent of the Johnson counties. Of thirty-two counties where Johnson polled 60 per cent or more of the two-party vote against Goldwater, Faubus polled as much against Rockefeller in fifteen counties. Johnson and Faubus ran better together particularly in non-Republican hill counties and in southern and southwestern counties. Johnson and Rockefeller ran better together particularly in non-Delta northeastern Arkansas. Only one county where Johnson got 60 per cent or more of the vote had a majority urban population, and Rockefeller carried it. It is doubtful that machine county politics had any significant effect on Johnson and Faubus running better together where they did.

How well did Goldwater run compared to Eisenhower and Nixon? Nixon carried twenty-three Arkansas counties in 1960; seventeen counties voted Republican in two of the three 1952-1960 presidential elections; and thirteen were Republican three times. Yet Goldwater carried only ten counties, and only four of these were Republican in all the elections 1952-1964, Sebastian, and three other hill counties. Of the other six Goldwater counties, one had voted Republican twice 1952-1960. Thus, while Goldwater made Republican a few southern Arkansas counties, he shrank the Republican base in northern and western Arkansas associated with Eisenhower and Nixon. Yet Eisenhower and Nixon Republicanism was essentially what Professor O. Douglas Weeks has called "the older mountain Republicanism or traditional Southern Republicanism."[95] The counties in which Fort Smith, Hot Springs, and Fayetteville are located supported Eisenhower and Nixon, but the flatter, heavier populated counties in which Little Rock and Pine Bluff are located gave neither candidate a plurality. Unlike in much of the South, what Weeks calls "Eisenhower-Nixon Republicanism" did not have a broad base in Arkansas, particularly in the non-hill urban counties, and thus there was less for Goldwater to lose. With more total votes cast in 1964, the Democratic plurality over Goldwater was greater than it had been since 1948, but the Republican vote was higher than in any 1948-1964 election. Goldwater's percentage of the two-party vote slipped 2.6 from 1960, yet it almost equaled Eisenhower's 1952 percentage.

Table 2 is based on a more detailed analysis of the 1964 vote in Pulaski County (Little Rock and North Little Rock) where census tract information is available and where voting areas can, at least in large part, be overlaid on census tract areas.[96]

In 1960 the two-party vote in Pulaski County was 54 per cent Democratic and 46 per cent Republican, about the same as for the state; but the total vote was 46.7 per cent Democratic, 39.7 per cent Republican, and 13.6 per cent National States Rights (Faubus). Pulaski County was twice as strong in States Rights support as the whole state, and 7,608 of the 28,952 States Rights votes in the state were polled there. In 1964 when the States Rights candidate polled only 442 votes in Pulaski, Johnson got only 51.4 per cent of the two-party vote, Goldwater got 48.6 per cent. There were 23,501 more votes cast in the 1964 presidential contest than in 1960, and a higher percentage of those who had poll tax receipts voted. There were 2,173 more votes cast in the 1964 gubernatorial race than in the presidential race, and Rockefeller got 53 per cent of the two-party vote.

A Negro-oriented Arkansas Voter Project, aided by the Southern Regional Council, worked in twenty-five counties and hoped to see that poll taxes had been paid for 100,000 of 190,000 potential Negro voters, so that the Negro vote might reach 25 per cent of the total.[97] The 100,000 goal was perhaps reached, but the Negro vote was probably only about 70,000 out of some 560,000 cast, so

TABLE 2

CHARACTERISTICS OF SELECTED CENSUS TRACTS IN THE LITTLE ROCK-
NORTH LITTLE ROCK AREA RANKED ACCORDING TO
JOHNSON VOTE, 1964

Tract Number	Johnson Percentage of Two-Party Vote, 1964	Kennedy Percentage of Total Vote, 1960	Faubus Percentage of Two-Party Vote, 1964	Percentage of 1960 Population Non-White	Median Family Income, 1959 In Dollars
2 LR	90.2	56.8	18.3	71.5	2870
28 NLR	89.4	—	20.8	96.6	2165
40 LR	87.8	50.4	18.2	94.1	2175
8 LR	84.5	53.0	20.7	92.5	2549
5 LR	79.7	44.4	23.4	73.5	3328
26 NLR	78.9	—	40.1	40.0	3339
29 NLR	59.2	—	54.6	48.0	3732
1 LR	53.6	56.0	56.9	7.7	3674
23 LR	44.3	47.6	41.6	a	7595
9 LR	42.2	49.8	65.3	a	3832
22 LR	42.0	38.2	34.9	1.6	8870
16 LR	39.1	36.8	36.5	1.5	10048
20 LR	38.0	44.0	45.9	a	7771

ᵃ Less than 1 per cent.

that only one-half of the 25 per cent goal was accomplished. However, Arkansas was one of those southern states with 45 per
cent or more Negro registration, all of which President Johnson
carried.[98] Johnson's Arkansas plurality was about the same as the
number of Negroes voting, therefore some election observers decided that the Negro vote carried Arkansas for Johnson. This type
of faulty analysis is too often engaged in. The truth is that if a
candidate carries a state, particularly in a close election, he has
no votes to spare, no matter where they come from. His plurality
comes from no particular area or group, even though his plurality
from one area or group coincides with his statewide plurality.
Nevertheless, the Negro vote was important to Johnson's victory
in Arkansas along with other complementary factors, including
Faubus's endorsement. And certainly the Pulaski County analysis
shows the extent of Johnson's Negro support. In that county sup-

posedly 9,000 Negro poll tax receipts were secured by the Arkansas Voter Project, and it was estimated that 16,000 of the some 79,000 votes cast for President there were Negro votes.[99] Table 2 reveals that in Pulaski voting areas Johnson's vote declined almost perfectly as did the Negro population. He improved his vote over Kennedy in Negro areas, but generally did less well in white areas.

Also, in Pulaski areas the Johnson vote decreased generally as income rose, but lower income white areas cut down Johnson's margins. In upper income white areas voters supported both Rockefeller and Goldwater, and Johnson generally ran better than Faubus. In the lower income white areas Faubus led Johnson percentage-wise, more so in one than the other. But it was in Negro areas that Johnson and Rockefeller secured similar percentages of the vote in their respective contests, as did Goldwater and Faubus, with Johnson and Rockefeller carrying the vote.

What meaning did the 1964 presidential election have for Republican hopes and the future? As noted above, Goldwater lost some counties which had been constant and dependable for the Republicans in the Eisenhower period, but he also gained a few counties. In essence, Goldwater did not gain much for presidential Republicanism in Arkansas, as might have been expected, yet he did not lose much for it either. Presidential Republicanism was still noticeable in Arkansas, but it had never won an election.

Perhaps real two-party politics will come to the state sooner through gubernatorial Republicanism, even though Rockefeller's percentage of the two-party vote was slightly less than Goldwater's (43 compared to 43.6). A revivified Arkansas Republican Party dates particularly from Winthrop Rockefeller's election as National Committeeman in 1961 and his eventual campaign for Governor. Both the 1962 and 1964 elections were described in terms of the greatest Republican efforts since Reconstruction. There was some depth in terms of candidates for lesser office in 1964 when 168 Republicans sought positions in the state, many of them candidates for Justice of the Peace, thirteen for County Judge, four for State Senator, and twenty-seven for State Representative.[100] But in neither election was there breadth or depth in victory. In 1964, apart from a few Justice of the Peace victories, Republicans reported the election of one State Representative, one County Treasurer, and one County Sheriff.[101]

At the state level Rockefeller Republicanism has been personality-oriented. Thus so-called two-party politics has characteristics of one-party Democratic primary election politics. In a state where Democratic politics has not shown a tendency to divide along liberal-conservative lines and stress policy differences, the Republican alternative has been more one of personality than of issue.[102] John R. Starr, Associated Press writer, reported that the 1964 Faubus-Rockefeller race ". . . lost many of its two-party aspects in a clash of personalities. The issues, too, were submerged in a wave of personal attacks. . . . The candidates were never far apart on the issues."[103] Perhaps there were more issue differences in the presidential race, but that contest was confusing with conservative Democrats supporting Johnson.

Whatever the electoral future of presidential or gubernatorial Republicanism in Arkansas, both or either may be instrumental in creating a genuine two-party system of meaningful alternatives, although more will be required than talk about a two-party system. Arkansas's political system may remain one-party and as confused as V. O. Key described it, longer than that of any other southern state, and real change will probably come from forces apart from political parties.

FOOTNOTES

[1] *Arkansas Gazette,* November 5, 1964.

[2] Republican National Committee, *Official Report of the Proceedings of the Twenty-seventh Republican National Convention* (Washington, D. C.: Republican National Committee, 1961); and *Arkansas Gazette,* May 22, 1964.

[3] Interview with Republican spokesman, May 18, 1964.

[4] *Arkansas Gazette,* May 17, 1964.

[5] *Ibid.,* May 22, 1964.

[6] *Ibid.,* July 16, 1964.

[7] *Ibid.,* and *Arkansas Democrat,* July 16, 1964.

[8] Democratic National Committee, *Official Report of the Proceedings of the 1960 Democratic National Convention and Committee* (Washington, D. C.: National Document Publishers, Inc., 1964); Democratic National Committee, *Temporary Roll of Delegates and Alternates to the Democratic National Convention, Atlantic City, New Jersey, August 22, 1964* (Washington, D. C.: Democratic National Committee, 1964); and Letter from Arkansas Democratic Chairman Leon B. Catlett to the writer, May 21, 1964.

[9] *Arkansas Gazette,* August 26 and 27, 1964.

[10] *Ibid.,* August 20, 1964.

[11] *Ibid.,* September 17, 1964.

[12] *Ibid.,* September 22 and August 11, 1964.

[13] *Ibid.,* September 20, 1964; and *W R Campaigner,* October 3, 1964.

[14] *Arkansas Gazette,* November 1, 1964.

[15] *Ibid.,* January 20, 1965.

[16] Interview with Republican worker, October 20, 1964.

[17] For estimates of headquarters and workers see *Northwest Arkansas Times,* September 30, 1964; and *Arkansas Gazette,* November 1, 1964.

[18] *Northwest Arkansas Times,* October 28, 1964.

[19] Information obtained from newspaper advertisements and the *Arkansas Gazette,* November 1, 1964.

[20] *Arkansas Gazette,* April 24, 1964.

[21] *Ibid.*, October 26 and 27, 1964.
[22] *Ibid.*, October 23, 1964.
[23] Interview with Young Democratic Club official, January, 1961.
[24] *Arkansas Gazette*, November 8, 1960.
[25] *Ibid.*, July 16, 1964.
[26] *Northwest Arkansas Times*, August 12, 1964; and *St. Louis Post-Dispatch*, August 15, 1964.
[27] Remarks at Democratic State Convention, 1962.
[28] Action of the Young Democratic Club Executive Board reported in the *Arkansas Gazette*, September 20, 1964.
[29] *Arkansas Gazette*, September 13, 1964.
[30] *Ibid.*, September 14, 1964.
[31] *Ibid.*, September 16, 20, and 21, 1964.
[32] *Arkansas Statesman*, September 24, 1964.
[33] *Arkansas Gazette*, September 26, 1964.
[34] *Ibid.*, October 10, 1964.
[35] See issues of the *Arkansas Statesman*, beginning with September 24, 1964.
[36] Interviews with party spokesmen, October 30 and November 6, 1964.
[37] *Arkansas Gazette*, September 19, 1964.
[38] *Ibid.*, September 24, 1964; and interview with party spokesman, October 30, 1964.
[39] Interview with party spokesman, October 30, 1964.
[40] *Arkansas Gazette*, November 1, 1964.
[41] *Ibid.*, July 17, 1964.
[42] *Ibid.*, October 13, 1964.
[43] *Ibid.*, October 19, 1964.
[44] See *The Democrat*, September 28, 1964; and the *Arkansas Gazette*, October 23, 1964.
[45] *Northwest Arkansas Times*, October 6, 1964.
[46] *Ibid.*, November 4, 1964; and *Arkansas Gazette*, November 1, 1964.
[47] *Arkansas Union Labor Bulletin*, October 9, 1964.
[48] *Arkansas Gazette*, November 1, 1964.
[49] *Ibid.*, September 17 and October 7, 1964; and interview with co-op official, February 23, 1965.
[50] *Arkansas Gazette*, October 8, 1964.
[51] Columnist Roy Reed, *Arkansas Gazette*, October 27, 1964.
[52] See Democratic News, September 8, 1964 as an example.
[53] *Arkansas Gazette*, October 9, 1964.
[54] *Special Campaign Bulletin No. 4: Faubus for Governor.*
[55] But the County Committee paid for newspaper advertisements urging voters to vote Democratic "all the way." See advertisement with Johnson's picture, "The Strongest Team in America," and advertisement with pictures of Johnson and Humphrey, "Keep The Democratic Team Working For You," in *Northwest Arkansas Times*, November 2, 1964.
[56] Letter from Benet D. Gellman, Regional Coordinator for the group, to the writer, September 24, 1964.
[57] As an example of local support of the national ticket the Pulaski County Committee sponsored "all the way" advertisements in the *Arkansas Gazette*. Individual office holders, such as the county clerk, circuit clerk, and county judge also urged national ticket support. See the *Arkansas Gazette*, October 31, 1964.
[58] *Arkansas Gazette*, September 17, 1964.
[59] *Ibid.*, October 15, 1964.
[60] *Ibid.*, September 19, 1964.
[61] *Ibid.*, September 26 and 27, 1964.
[62] *Ibid.*, October 28, 1964.
[63] See pamphlets entitled *Add Up The Score* and *Partners In Progress.*
[64] *Arkansas Gazette*, October 16, 1964.
[65] See statement of State Chairman Catlett in the *Arkansas Gazette*, October 7, 1964.
[66] See *Gazette* advertisement, October 28, 1964.
[67] *Arkansas Gazette* editorial, October 8, 1964.
[68] *Arkansas Gazette*, October 20, 1964.
[69] *Ibid.*, November 5, 1964.

70 *Ibid.,* October 1, 1964.
71 *Arkansas Gazette* editorial, October 19, 1964.
72 *Arkansas Gazette,* October 28, 1964.
73 Arkansas for Goldwater Committee advertisement in *Southwest American,* October 28, 1964.
74 *Arkansas Gazette,* November 2, 1964, and other state newspapers.
75 *Arkansas Democrat,* October 27, 1964.
76 Advertisement in *Gazette,* November 2, 1964.
77 *Arkansas Gazette,* September 16, 1964.
78 *Ibid.,* October 22, 1964.
79 *Ibid.,* November 1, 1964.
80 *Ibid.,* October 1 and November 1, 1964.
81 See *Gazette,* November 1, 1964.
82 The circulation of the *Gazette* is about 97,000, that of the *Democrat* about 86,000, that of their closest competitor about 21,000.
83 *Arkansas Gazette,* November 1, 1964.
84 In the 1964 general election voters approved a state constitutional amendment setting up a voter registration system.
85 *Northwest Arkansas Times,* October 6, 1964.
86 Based on Associated Press analysis in *St. Louis Post-Dispatch,* November 11, 1964.
87 *Arkansas Gazette,* September 17 and October 27, 1964.
88 State vote figures cited in this writing were provided by the Secretary of State for 1964. Pulaski County figures were copied from voting records in the County Clerk's Office. The source of 1948 figures is George Gallup, *The Political Almanac: 1952* (New York: B. C. Forbes and Sons Inc., 1952). Figures for other presidential elections are based on the *America Votes* volumes edited by Richard M. Scammon. Reference is usually to the two-party, Democratic-Republican vote. If a third party has polled a significant vote particularly, reference may be to the total vote cast.
89 The ten Goldwater counties (his two-party percentage ranging from 56.3 in Ashley to 51.2 in Carroll) were: Ashley, Sebastian, Howard, Union, Arkansas, Columbia, Searcy, Drew, Benton, and Carroll.
90 Information on geography, agriculture, and soil was obtained from Professor Lyell Thompson, Agronomy Department, College of Agriculture, University of Arkansas.
91 The source for population and income figures is U. S. Bureau of the Census, *County and City Data Book, 1962.*
92 In addition to the ten counties Goldwater carried he polled at least 45% of the two-party vote in fourteen counties: Bradley, Cleveland, Crawford, Crittenden, Cross, Dallas, Garland, Lafayette, Lonoke, Miller, Monroe, Newton, Pulaski, and St. Francis.
93 Both candidates carried Benton, Carroll, Searcy, and Sebastian counties. Goldwater carried in addition Ashley, Howard, Union, Arkansas, Columbia, and Drew counties. Rockefeller carried in addition Boone, Marion, Baxter, Washington, Pulaski and Jefferson counties.
94 *New York Times,* November 5, 1964.
95 O. Douglas Weeks, "The Prospects of the Republican Party in the South," *Public Affairs Comment* (Institute of Public Affairs, the University of Texas), XI, No. 1 (January, 1965).
96 U. S. Bureau of the Census, *U. S. Censuses of Population and Housing: 1960. Census Tracts* (Final Report PHC (1) - 80). An exact overlay of voting areas on a census tract area is not always possible; therefore some tracts were not used, and in some cases the vote estimate of each candidate in a tract area will be less than exact.
97 *New York Times,* August 12, 1964; and *Arkansas Gazette,* September 27, 1964.
98 *New York Times,* November 22, 1964.
99 *Arkansas Gazette,* October 22 and November 16, 1964.
100 *Ibid.,* November 1, 1964.
101 *Arkansas GOP Outlook,* December 1, 1964.
102 In spite of its vintage, V. O. Key, Jr., *Southern Politics in State and Nation* (New York: Alfred A. Knopf Inc., 1949), Chapter 9, remains a highly accurate account of Arkansas's political system. The writer does not feel that Faubus Era politics would force much revision of Key. Of what other southern state could this now be said?
103 *Northwest Arkansas Times,* November 2, 1964.

The 1964 Election in Louisiana: An Example of Ethnic Politics In the South

KENNETH N. VINES*

Tulane University

This paper presents an analysis of the presidential election of 1964 in the state of Louisiana. Through the use of aggregate political and social data gathered for the parishes, it compares the results of the election with previous national elections and relates election results to other social data. By this kind of analysis we can describe more fully the character of elections and can also compare electoral patterns with different voting results and with a variety of social and economic data. The analysis or aggregate data are particularly suited to the description and analysis of elections and enables us to place a given election in its social and political setting and to establish electoral patterns of several dimensions, patterns across time and those that reveal special social and political features.

The particular advantages and liabilities concerned with the use of aggregate data have already been stated.[1] While it is dangerous to rely on aggregate data for generalizations concerning personal behavior, the analysis of electoral patterns and the study of electoral institutions are entirely suitable. The familiar propositions concerning the nature of social collectives are assumed here. These unorganized groups consist of families and individuals tied by shared traditions and common perspectives. Consensus is held tacitly, remains largely latent, and is revealed only under certain conditions or when stimuli bring it about. These assumptions inhere in our division of Louisiana into socio-cultural areas such as north Louisiana, south Louisiana, different Negro-White population areas, and urban-rural divisions.[2]

Background of the 1964 election

Usually classified as one of the "Deep South" states of the Confederacy, Louisiana actually has a diversity of political tend-

* I wish to acknowledge the aid of Joseph Walker, graduate student in Political Science, who allowed me access to his collection of data, and Joel Mendler, undergraduate student in Political Science, who wrote a paper on the 1964 election in Louisiana.

encies within its borders. Deep South politics is best represented by the northern portion of the state which is made up of parishes where social and political tendencies of the deep south predominate. These consist of a large Negro population, reliance on tenancy relationships in the agricultural system, existence of the historical system of cotton plantation economy, and a general maintenance of the political and social values of a segregated society. By contrast somewhat different tendencies are embodied in some north central parishes of the state where the political movements identified as "Longism" originated. These parishes have low Negro populations, small farms in cut-over areas, and a predilection for populist politics. But both sections are overwhelmingly Protestant-Anglo-Saxon in population and rarely see Catholics.

Setting Louisiana apart from its Deep South neighbors is a socially and politically significant group of parishes in the southwestern part of the state. These parishes form the main body of French-Catholic Louisiana, a slight misnomer since a small number of other ethnic Catholic groups are mixed in the population. The parishes vary in the percentage of Negro population and depend upon a varied agricultural base, consisting of such crops as rice, sugar cane, and garden crops. The Catholic ethnic groups of southwestern Louisiana differ from the Catholic groups of the northern United States in their relationship to historical culture. While Catholic ethnic groups in the North (mostly recent immigrants) were late arrivals to the society, Louisiana Catholics are the old residents of Louisiana and in most cases were on hand to welcome the Anglo-Saxon-Protestant immigrants who came to Louisiana.

As in the South in general, the Republican presidential vote has risen rapidly since 1940, with an especially large increase in the 1952 election. In the election of 1956 Eisenhower carried the state. The election of 1960 brought an abrupt halt to the development of the Republican presidential vote when Kennedy's large majority demonstrated the potential political appeal of Catholic candidates to the voters of the state. With the exception of the 1960 election, however, the Republican presidential vote has been competitive in the state's recent presidential politics.

Relation of the 1964 election to other recent elections

The election of 1964 marked the second time (also 1956) Louisiana voted for Republican candidates and the third time the state failed to support the Democratic party (in 1948 the state cast its vote for the States' Rights candidate). Louisiana was one of five Deep South states that voted Republican in 1964 (the other four were Alabama, Georgia, Mississippi, and South Carolina), and four of these (excepting Georgia) voted for the States' Rights candidate in the election of 1948. Among the Deep South states there has been a certain consistency of electoral behavior: namely, they respond in a generally similar fashion to the stimuli of national presidential elections.

But the character of the 1964 elections results, the size of the national Democratic majority, and the collapse of national Republican voting strength suggest that there may have been some special circumstances at work so that the election may not have been a continuation of past electoral patterns. Table 1 presents data for the examination of these propositions.

Table 1 compares the parish votes for the Republican and States Rights' nominees in the four preceding elections with the Republican vote for the election of 1964. The comparison indicates that the 1964 election was not a deviant election, different in the

TABLE 1

CORRELATION OF 1964 REPUBLICAN VOTE FOR PRESIDENT WITH REPUBLICAN AND STATES' RIGHTS VOTE FOR PRESIDENT FROM 1948-1960 IN THE PARISHES OF LOUISIANA*

Year	Vote	Coefficient of Correlation
1948	R	—.471
	SR	.426
	RSR	.241
1952	R	.392**
1956	R	—.267
	SR	.697
	RSR	.618
1960	R	.631
	SR	.798
	RSR	.957

* Legend: R is Republican vote, SR is States' Rights vote, and RSR is the Republican and States' Rights vote combined. Coefficients are simple Pearsonian correlations.

** The States' Rights party did not appear on the Louisiana ballot in 1952.

character of its voting patterns from previous elections; indeed, it was a continuation of important trends firmly established in the presidential voting of Louisiana.

The most important correspondence—and a striking one it is—is the relation of the Goldwater vote with the combined Republican and States' Rights vote for the 1960 elections. The correlation of .957 accounts for very nearly all the variance and indicates an extremely close relationship. The evidence suggests, accordingly, that the sources of the Goldwater vote may be located in close promimity to the sources of the Republican and States' Rights vote of the previous election. In 1960 the Republican-States' Rights vote was outweighed by the favorable response to the Kennedy candidacy. In 1964 the sources that produced the Republican-States' Rights vote in 1960 combined to support the Republican party and proportionately increased the vote over the 1960 total to carry Louisiana easily for the Republicans. The important point is, however, that although the Goldwater vote was much larger than the Republican-States' Rights vote of 1960, the Republican vote in 1964 was a proportionate increase in size closely related to its balance with the Democratic vote of 1960—hence the extremely high correlation of .957. The close correspondence strongly suggests, therefore, that the Goldwater vote had its source in an increased extension of the combined Republican-States' Rights vote of 1960.

The data also suggested several other conclusions concerning the relationship of the Goldwater vote with recent presidential votes in Louisiana. The States' Rights vote in recent elections correlates rather strongly with the Republican presidential vote of 1964; .798 in 1960, .697 in 1956, and .426 in 1948. This relationship hints that the States' Rights vote, taken alone, was an important element in the Goldwater support and turned out to contribute to the Republican majority of 1964.

With the Republican votes of the elections preceding 1960, the support identified with Eisenhower Republicanism, the relationships are not close, for support for the Republican party in 1964 seems not to correspond with the support in 1956 and 1952, and to be quite different from the Republican vote in 1948. Generally, the Republican party in Louisiana has passed through three stages of development. Prior to 1952, predominant support for the party came from the "sugar bowl parishes," those parishes in the southwestern part of the state specializing in sugar cane crops. The sugar parishes were irritated over Democratic permissiveness toward sugar tariffs in the 1890's, and in a gesture of exasperation many of the sugar planters and their supporters went over to the Republican party in presidential elections. This tradition of Republican support continued through the election of 1948 and constituted the state's most important source of Republican strength up until the advent of Eisenhower Republicanism. The elections of 1952 and 1956 brought the enthusiasm for Republican development under the leadership of Eisenhower, an enthusiasm especially marked in the urban areas, moderate on racial issues and identified with the building of a two-party system. Later, the character of Republican support in Louisiana is not clear but seems to have become identified in the election of 1960 with anti-Catholic reactions and with a less moderate stance on racial issues. These changes in the Republican party are reflected in Table 1. The Goldwater vote actually correlates negatively with the Republican vote in 1948 and in 1956, and shows only a slight positive relationship in 1952; in 1960, however, there is a moderately high correlation with the Republican vote in that election.

Sources of Democratic support

In the comparison of election returns we have suggested that the Republican victory in Louisiana in 1964 was a continuation of trends already pronounced in the presidential politics of 1960. The presidential elections of 1960 and 1964 involved, however, marked departures from the patterns evident in the elections during the candidacies of Eisenhower. Having compared general patterns of political support among the parishes, a further analysis of the elections in the context of other social and political features is necessary.

A look at the character of Democratic support in recent elections reveals several prominent features of Democratic strength in Louisiana. First, like the Republican support, the nature of Democratic support in the parishes is closely related to the Democratic vote of 1960 but, unlike the Republican vote, rather strongly corresponds to the vote in the election of 1956. Table 2 indicates the extremely close correspondence between the elections of 1960 and 1964. The Democratic vote in 1956 is also rather closely related to the 1964 vote, but the relationship is not as close as the 1960-64 one. Also slightly related to the 1964 vote is the Democratic support in 1952. A possible reason for the closer relationship of the 1956 vote than the 1952 one is the

102   THE 1964 PRESIDENTIAL ELECTION

TABLE 2

COMPARISON OF 1964 DEMOCRATIC VOTE FOR PRESIDENT WITH
DEMOCRATIC PRESIDENTIAL VOTE IN THE ELECTIONS OF
1948-60 IN THE PARISHES OF LOUISIANA

Year	Vote	Coefficient of Correlation
1948	Democratic	.241
1952	Democratic	.392
1956	Democratic	.618
1960	Democratic	.957

presence in the 1956 election of a States' Rights candidate. The
States' Rights candidate had the function, we might speculate,
of drawing off the segregationist vote so that in that election the
resultant vote is largely moderate on race relations issues and
so correlates more closely with the non-segregationist Democratic
candidacy of 1964.

The consistency of Democratic support in Louisiana from one
election to another in recent times suggests that Democratic
strength can be located primarily in a group of high Democratic
parishes. For example, Johnson carried 23 parishes in 1964, and
all of these parishes were high Democratic in 1960 and with
certain important exceptions in 1956 as well. Table 3 compares
the ranking of the fifteen highest Democratic parishes in 1964
with their rank in Democratic support for the two previous
elections.

The French-Catholic ethnic influence

To label the French Catholics who largely constitute the population of southwest Louisiana as "ethnics" is, in one sense, highly
presumptuous. After all, the French Catholics were the original
settlers of the state, and their influence is deeply rooted in Louisiana's social and political institutions. There are several reasons,
however, why it is useful to speak of the French-Catholics as
members of an ethnic population. First, the Catholic population
has remained relatively segregated in the southwest parishes of
Louisiana, and their identity has been maintained as a contrast to
the Protestant Anglo-Saxons of the northern part of the state.[3] The
ethnic conception of French Catholics also links them with more
recent ethnic populations of the United States with whom they
may have much in common and share social and political re-

TABLE 3

COMPARATIVE RANKINGS OF FIFTEEN HIGHEST
DEMOCRATIC PARISHES IN ELECTIONS FROM 1956-64

Parish	1964 Rank	1960 Rank	1956 Rank	Rank in Catholic Population
St. James	1	2	15	High
Vermillion	2	6	10	High
St. John	3	4	16	High
Lafourche	4	7	34	High
St. Martin	5	5	8	High
St. Charles	6	15	31	High
Cameron	7	1	4	High
Evangeline	8	3	3	High
Ascension	9	10	7	High
Jefferson Davis	10	15	36	High
Acadia	11	9	5	High
Assumption	12	16	29	High
Allen	13	20	17	High
Calcasieu	14	18	18	High
St. Mary	15	19	35	High
St. Helena	----	----	1	Low
Livingston	----	----	2	Low-Medium
Washington	----	----	6	Low
East Feliciana	----	----	9	Low

sponses. We may hypothesize that political values that stir ethnic populations of the North, candidates with ethnic identities and issues sensitive to ethnic populations, all awaken similar responses in the French-Catholics of Louisiana.

Taken as a whole the correspondence between Catholic population and Democratic voting in the elections of 1960 and 1964 has been high.

TABLE 4

CORRELATION BETWEEN PER CENT CATHOLIC CHURCH MEMBERSHIP
AND DEMOCRATIC VOTE IN 1960-1964 IN LOUISIANA PARISHES

Year	Correlation
1960	.841
1964	.741

Table 4 is based upon the rough data of the 1936 census for the religious population of the parishes. The data are now ambiguous for expressing religious differences not only because of age but also because of the inaccuracies in the techniques employed for compilation. Nevertheless, it remains our best source of statewide religious population information—especially if we assume that religious populations have a tendency to reproduce themselves over a period of time and that there have been relatively few mass populations movements in the state as a whole. Our confidence in the data is somewhat strengthened by the close relationships it produces with certain social and political events when we would expect close relationships. Notably, strong correlations are produced, using the 1936 religious census data, when we compare variations among the Catholic population in the state with the Democratic vote in the parishes. We would expect just such strong correlations as those indicated for the elections of 1960 and 1964. Certain state elections featuring Catholic candidates have produced similar results.

The importance of French-Catholic parishes in the constitution of the Democratic vote may be inferred from Table 4. All 23 parishes that supported the Democrats in 1964 were high in Catholic population and, to a large extent, these parishes were the highest Democratic ranking parishes in 1960, as a comparison of the 15 highest Democratic parishes of 1964 indicates. In 1956 there was a tendency for the high Democratic parishes of the two previous elections to rank high in Democratic support, but there were two groups of parishes that deviated from this pattern. Five parishes that ranked toward the middle of the partisan distribution in 1956 (Lafourche, St. Charles, Jefferson Davis, Assumption, and St. Mary) had increased Democratic support in 1960 and 1964 to become high ranking Democratic areas. The sudden increase in support may be explained by the abandonment of sugar-tariff related support of Republican candidates in favor of responses to the Catholic-ethnic character of the Kennedy candidacy—all five parishes are located in the state's sugar bowl and also have large Catholic populations. Four other parishes (St. Helena, Livingston, Washington, and East Feliciana) that ranked quite high in Democratic support for the election of 1956 fell below the state Democratic average in the two succeeding elections and were displaced from the ranks of high Democratic parishes. Low Catholic populations are present in these parishes and the candidacy of Kennedy evoked a decline in Democratic support that remained in the 1964 election.

While the roots of Democratic support in the French Catholic parishes may be observed in the 1956 election, it is clear that the Catholic candidacy of Kennedy brought large numbers of Louisiana Catholic voters to the Democratic party. Moreover, the election returns suggest that the effects of the Kennedy candidacy outlasted the immediate election in which it was involved and affected the Johnson-Goldwater contest. We suspect that the Kennedy candidacy suggested highly favorable perceptions of the Democratic party to the French Catholics and these favorable images remained to influence the choice of candidates in the 1964 election. Quite likely, Louisiana Catholics were influenced by the same factors that drew ethnic populations in the remainder of the nation to the Democratic party in the late '20's and early '30's. John Kennedy probably kindled old memories of ethnic identification with the Democratic party and refurbished ancient party loyalties. In support of this contention, the election of 1928 exhibits the closest parallel in electoral patterns of support to the contests of 1960 and 1964. Louisiana gave Smith overwhelming support coming largely from the French Catholic parishes and thus deviated from the remainder of the South where Democratic majorities were greatly reduced.

The moderate attitude of French Catholic populations toward the politics of race relations makes possible support of Democratic presidential candidates espousing civil rights. Although the Catholic parishes are part of the state segregation system and live in a segregated society, some evidence indicates that the people in these parishes hold more moderate attitudes toward such questions as racial segregation and Negro voter registration than do Protestant Anglo-Saxon peoples who inhabit the northern part of the state.[4] In consequence, French Catholic voters are not deterred to the same extent as other Louisiana voters from supporting Democratic candidates identified with civil rights doctrines. Louisiana's ethnic voters were thus able to support both Kennedy and Johnson as Democratic candidates; the non-Catholic parishes in the north appear, on the other hand, to have reacted against both the ethnic associations of the Democratic party and its linkages with civil rights issues.

The Effects of Negro-White Population Balance

Of all the variables in southern social life presumed to affect the outcomes of southern politics, probably the best known is the Negro-White population balance—the percentage of Negroes in the total population. The presumption is—fortified by impressive evidence—that those areas with large Negro populations react differently in political situations from those with small Negro populations. This theory presumes that areas with a large balance of Negroes support those candidates and factions most likely to maintain the racial status quo and least likely to support change in favor of national values. The Goldwater candidacy identified with support of the status quo as contrasted with the more positive position of Johnson on civil rights might be predicted to bring out support for the Republican party in those areas with large Negro populations.

Examining the overall correspondence between per cent Negro population and Republican vote, we find that the rank correlation is +.38. Since the coefficient of correlation indicates only overall relations and does not show sub-categories which may be related, a further analysis of the two variables is needed. As it is, the correlation of .38 indicates a relationship only slightly significant, and we are curious to discover why the variables are not more closely related as we might expect.

TABLE 5

RELATION OF PER CENT NEGRO POPULATION TO REPUBLICAN VOTE
OF 1964 IN THREE AREAS OF LOUISIANA

Area	% Negro	% Republican Vote	No. of Parishes
Northern Louisiana	12.7-27.8	71.1	8
	30.5-36.8	70.9	8
	40.6-49.4	75.6	8
	50.3-65.0	82.0	5
French-Catholic	6.4-24.8	45.2	11
Louisiana	26.8-37.4	48.2	9
	41.2-53.6	43.1	7
Florida Parishes	15.0-27.5	56.4	2
	31.8-33.9	58.0	3
	54.0-66.1	76.7	3

Table 5 indicates that in the north Louisiana parishes and in the Florida parishes (those situated in the eastern part of the state and so-called because of their inclusion in the original Florida territory) the Republican vote tends to rise as the percentage of Negroes increases and especially so in the Florida parishes. There is little relationship between Negro-White population balance and Goldwater support, however, in the French-Catholic parishes. While the percentage of Negro population in French Louisiana is not quite as high as some of the 60 per cent levels reached by a few parishes in the non-southern sections, the levels of Negro population in seven of the Catholic parishes is over 40 per cent and is over half the population in several parishes. We may conclude that differences in Negro population significantly affect partisan support in parishes in north and east Louisiana but make little difference in French Catholic parishes.

The impression of differential affects of Negro populations upon election patterns in north Louisiana is strengthened by an inspection of the group of northern parishes that gave Johnson his highest vote. In no case did the Democratic vote amount to a majority, but the group of nine parishes ranked considerably above their northern neighbors and in several, for example Beauregard and Vernon, the election was close. Five of the six highest have low Negro populations and (with the one exception of Jackson Parish) are located in the same economic region of the northern rural part of Louisiana. In this region a low rate of tenancy goes along with the low Negro population and the farming consists of small crops and livestock production. These parishes are politically interesting because they constituted much of the bulwark of support for Huey Long and his successors who carried out the spirit of his policies.

The Effects of Urbanism

The development of southern Republican support during the Eisenhower period focused attention on the cities as loci of special Republican support. By and large the urban centers in the South furnished the Republican votes that brought the South a competitive party politics for presidential elections, and, indeed, furnished electoral votes in some southern states in all elections since 1952.

Table 6 indicates that parishes with different urban characteristics differed only insignificantly in their partisan support in the 1964 election. Moreover, looking at urban differences alone, there were not consistent differences among high and low urban places.

TABLE 6

RELATIONSHIP BETWEEN PER CENT URBAN AND REPUBLICAN VOTE
IN PRESIDENTIAL ELECTION OF 1964 IN THREE AREAS OF LOUISIANA

Area	% Urban	% Republican (Average)	No. of Parishes
Northern Parishes	0.0-15.5	81.0	9
	17.0-27.6	73.3	6
	37.5-52.6	72.1	9
	57.2-80.8	80.9	5
French-Catholic	0.0-25.7	40.6	7
Parishes	33.0-41.5	41.7	9
	47.9-59.4	43.0	5
Florida Parishes	0.0-00.1	76.7	3
	22.2-35.7	56.5	2
	55.8-85.1	58.3	2

Instead the data confirm that regional differences were more important than urban/rural ones, for French Catholic parishes whether rural or urban supported the Democrats at a correspondingly higher rate than did the corresponding parishes in northern Louisiana.

An inspection of the seven largest cities in Louisiana—New Orleans, Monroe, Baton Rouge, Lafayette, Shreveport, Lake Charles and Alexandria—reveals little change from the general pattern of urban/rural support. Taken as a whole the group of largest cities, all with populations over 75,000, supported the candidacy of Goldwater by a margin of 226,148 votes to 169,099. The amount of support varied according to the location of the city, however, with those in south Louisiana voting for Johnson and those in the north supporting Goldwater. The contrast between percentage support of cities in north and south Louisiana is shown in Table 7.

In the large urban areas, particularly, the distinction between French Catholic and non-French Catholic populations is blurred in part because of movements in and out of the city, noticeably in the case of New Orleans where the Catholic population is now only slightly more than half the total religious population. The likelihood is, however, that the cities of north Louisiana have received little additions of Catholic population.

TABLE 7

COMPARISON OF DEMOCRATIC VOTE IN NORTH AND SOUTH LOUISIANA
CITIES IN 1964 PRESIDENTIAL ELECTION

Area	Parish	City	% Democratic
North	Caddo	Shreveport	19.4
	East Baton Rouge	Baton Rouge	42.2
	Ouachita	Monroe	19.4
	Rapides	Alexandria	35.3
South	Calcasieu	Lake Charles	57.9
	Lafayette	Lafayette	53.4
	Orleans	New Orleans	50.3

Conclusions

The politics of Louisiana offers the sole important example of the influence of ethnic groups in southern electoral politics. While there are scattered isolani of ethnic influence throughout the remainder of the South, for example a few Germanic counties in south central Texas and one county (Winston) in north central Alabama, in no other state has the influence of an ethnic group been as distinctive or substantial as the French Catholics in Louisiana.

Recent presidential elections illustrate the continuing influence of the French Catholics and their effect on presidential electoral patterns. After a number of important variables were considered, the most durable effects appeared in the religio-cultural character of the population. While the factor of Negro-White population balance was related to the strength of Goldwater support in the northern part of the state, the percentage of Negroes appeared not to be related to partisan patterns in the southern part of the state. These relationships suggest, as do some other evidence, that in Louisiana the religio-cultural character of the populations was more strongly related to the character of partisan support than other social and political features.

The manner in which ethnic features are related to Democratic support, we suppose, is similar to the involvement of ethnic populations with the Democratic partisan support outside the South. Both the 1928 and the 1960 elections brought forth enthusiastic support for Catholic candidates in Louisiana that offered a contrast to the responses of the remainder of the South. Democratic support among the Louisiana Catholics appears to have persisted from the 1960 election to the subsequent election even though no Catholic candidacies were involved. In this sense the Louisiana groups reflected the responses that national ethnic and religious groups made to the election. In Louisiana, however, the Democratic support was not sufficient to overcome the overwhelming opposition from other state groups, and hence the Louisiana ethnics did not carry the day for their candidate.

FOOTNOTES

[1] See among others: W. S. Robinson, "Ecological Correlations and the Behavior of Individuals," *American Sociological Review*, Vol. XV, June 1950, pp. 351-57; Austin Ranney, "The Utility and Limitations of Aggregate Data in the Study of Electoral Behavior," Austin Ranney (ed.) *Essays on the Behavioral Study of Politics* (Urbana: University of Illinois Press, 1962).

[2] See Perry Howard, *Political Tendencies in Louisiana, 1812-1952* (Baton Rouge, Louisiana State University Studies No. 5, 1957).

[3] *Ibid.*

[4] John Fenton and Kenneth N. Vines, "Negro Registration in Louisiana," *American Political Science Review*, Vol. LI, September 1957, pp. 704-14.

B
I
N